The First Congregational Church,
Methuen, Mass.

The Second Meeting House

A
Short History of the
First Church
of
Methuen, Mass.
(1729-1929)

by
Frederick D. Hayward

SicPress 2013
Methuen, Mass.

A Short History of the First Church and Parish of Methuen, Massachusetts (1729-1929) by Frederick D. Hayward was published in by The Methuen Press in 1929 in Methuen, Massachusetts.

series edited by J. Godsey
sales@SicPress.com
Methuen, MA 2013

TABLE OF CONTENTS

AUTHOR'S PREFACE

To sketch the life of a New England church extending through two centuries of continual existence is a task worthy of more than passing notice. To the casual reader the matter of putting together names and events wrung from books and papers may appear a task not the greatest. We accept the decision, and yet if such be the case, we must confess that to peruse old fragmentary yellow pages of records and diaries penned in a hand not easily decipherable and through which the phonetic method of spelling too often held full sway, is not by any means other than a work needing special care and attention.

Let the reader understand the writer. The work has been a continual joy. Often a discovery has been made giving a real thrill. An education in itself comes to him who thus carefully assembles facts gleaned from the changing eras.

We are delving into books written by the hand of two centuries. Years in which men came to new homes from a vast New England wilderness; in which every step of the church was one of the town itself; into which life came wars long and severe; struggle with the native red-skins of these forests; with the great ancestral powers of the eastern world; with men of their own blood during the trying days of '61-'65. Year of change in the religious life; in the political; in the civil, when men of the village and town were to build cities destined to produce problems new and disturbing. Years in which men were to realize an independence for which they had long fought and died. Years in which new industries were to arise and from which years was to emerge a new life built upon the old; in which we live and for which we should as well give our due thanks.

This old church celebrating its advanced birthday thus speaks. That the reader may listen is the hope of one who has faithfully read its pages and now offers their contents. Let it be well understood that the material contained in the following chapters was practically obtained from the records themselves. Many thanks are due fellow townsmen and members of the church and parish for countless items given. And yet, not one thus received has been used in this work without first "checking up" the same from some historic book or paper. It has been our good fortune to have access to practically all records of both first and second parishes with the exception of some thirty years of the first parish in which the complete records of the church for that period supplied the gap.

Again expressing thanks due the many scions of the early years for the many items of interest given; as well to the countless friends who have encouraged their historian to keep continually at his task also to the readers who may patiently overlook the countless mistakes that must necessarily creep into such a work, the writer modestly hands to the church what he has endeavored to produce is the truth regarding a long life which none can deny has been one replete with tasks well done.

—ONE—

The inception of our New England social and civic life had the religious as a basis. It is nigh unto the impossible to write of the development of colonial affairs in this north-eastern section of our country without placing it on a common plane of man's devotion to his Creator. Correspondingly, true, it is that that in sketching the beginnings and progress of the church we are constantly in touch with matters civil.

The history of our local church is no exception to this rule. Methuen was built upon the church. The life of the latter is closely identified with the progress of the town. The "meeting house" and the minister were supported by a "rate" even distinct from that levied upon the township as a whole. During the first year of Methuen's life half a score of town meetings were held the principal business of which was the arrangement for religious services. At a town meeting held

> March ye 9, 1725-6 voted that the select men should have power to agree with an athodoxt minester for ye year insuing and not to exceed five and forty pounds and find the minester his diat.

In this vote, we find several facts worthy mention. We see clearly that the town as a whole was responsible, through its selectmen, for the welfare of the new church, which custom continued until 1778. The original grant by the General Court, "Anno Regni Regis Georgii Duodecimo," contained among other provisions the one that a period of three years was allowed the petitioners to establish the new town and "settle a learned orthodox minister of good conversation." The selectmen were to arrange for the fulfillment of these conditions. Again, the continued meetings anew, the question would indicate that the whole matter became real business proposition.

9

Until the meeting-house could become a fact, – (and we all know of the trials and tribulations attending its location and erection) – services were to be held at the home of Asie Swan; probably located on what we now know as Ferry St. in Lawrence. Some months later an attempt was made to move the place of worship to the home of James Howe; near the Edward Taylor farm on our Howe Street. But no, Swan was a leader in town affairs; especially in this eastern section bound to be somewhat at odds with the west part undoubtedly settled or rather occupied many years previous. Indeed we read that in 1726-7 the call for the annual greeting was by "posting up the warrant on ye doore of Asie Swan's house."

We shall not burden the reader with the oft-told story of the dispute between the east and west factions; (the latter led by Stephen Barker.) Nor shall we tell of the frame erected on what we now know as Powder House Hill and, later by order of the General Court moved to "Daddy Frye's Hill", (now so called), near the junction of East and Berkeley streets. Let us pass over the details and state that on August 28, 1728, the meeting-house was completed and its doors thrown open for the civic and religious affairs of the new town. Here in this building for sixty-eight years, the good of Methuen listened to the word of God, as preached twice each Sabbath—as well, were the affairs regarding civil and political issues of state and nation freely discussed and justly settled. In 1796, a second house was erected on the same site. In 1832 this second building was moved to the site of our present stone edifice; a monument of New Hampshire granite which "dominated the village" as said Bishop Lawrence in his *Memories of a Happy Life* (p. 44.) This third meeting-house, our present place of worship, was dedicated October 3, 1855; but more of this later.

Within the time limit as designated by the Court, (with but a few months to spare), the First Parish Methuen became a reality. That "athodoxt" ministers had been secured is evidenced by occasional references in the town book of records to money "allowed" different men for "preaching." A Mr. Heath appears to have been the first named in this list. On April 10, 1727, "forty pounds money" was voted to be paid him, "for his work in the ministry the year past and for his year's diat & candels fifteen pounds." At this same meeting it was also voted "that the selectmen should provide a place for the mienester to be honourable etertained & Boarded att". On the following December 4, the annals tell us that a Mr. Walker was paid six pounds five shillings money "for the present year he preached here." At this time the name of Mr. Sargent first appears. He is to be paid forty-three pounds fifteen shillings, his salary during the time he was with them. There may have been other candidates but these are the only ones found in the records.

Mr. Christopher Sargent evidently was the choice of the people for their minister. The fact that he had supplied the pulpit for some months would indicate this. On March 3, 1729, a formal "call" was extended him; "to Dispense the word of God to us." At the same time a committee was appointed to make all arrangements, as to "work" and 'terms"- "he will setel upon" and to report at the "Annual Meeting in this Instant March."

Before we approach the discussion regarding the new pastor's salary, as well as the creation of the church as distinct from the parish, and the great day of ordination; let us pause at this point, to describe the territory originally assigned by the mother town Haverhill, as a parsonage for the new church to be.

–TWO–

ALLOTMENT AND LOCATION OF PARSONAGE-LANDS.

In the town book of records under the date of Feb. 17, 1728-9, we read the following:

We the subscribers have land out one piece of land more lying northward from the world's end pond: for a parsonage for this town containing about seventy acre which makes up our parsonages. According to the order of the General Court, and is bounded as followeth, viz: first with a small Black oak tree marked with the letter P standing by Carlton's Road & from thence south-westward to a pine marked with the letar P, and from thence to the Bounds first laid out by Joshua Swan, James Davis, and Daniel Bodwel, comtee to lay out sd land.

According to the records, this was recorded on March 3, 1728-9. A record of just ten days later is also carefully preserved and reads as follow:

(P)ursuant to the town's vote we the subscribers have vewed Sr survayed the pats sonage land In this town which was laid out by the town of Haverhill for the use of the minestry for the west end of the town of Haverhill, but now in Methuen laying where our meeting house Now stands and whare our Buring place is laid out and we find that there is about seventy acers of said parsonage: and also we have laid two pieces more to mak up ouer parsonage. According to the order of the General Court. one piece lying on The easterly side of Bare medow containing about sixty acers And is bounded as followeth: beginning with a pine tree marken on the easterly side of Bare medow, and so Running easterly to another pine marked standing by the Road that leads from Whittier's land to muscato Bridg & so Bounded By sd Road until it comes to another pine tree standing by sd Road on the side of an hill near sd Bridg and so southerly to a pine which is a bound of Capt. James Frys land and so southwesterly to another pine tree standing by the parth that leads from William Whittiers to John Croases which is a bound of said Fryes land And so northwesterly to a Read oak tree marked standing on the north side of an hill next to Bare medow, and from thence to the Bound first mentioned laid out by Joshua Swan, James Davis & Daniel Bodwel Cometie to lay out sd land.

We find that the above was duly recorded by William Whittier, Town Clark March 6, 1728-9. The reader will notice that these plots of land, laid out under the direction of the town, as ordered by the Court, constituted the original two hundred acres. Should we go back a few years it would appear that these grants constituted the concession to the request for a separate existence from the mother town, Haverhill. Such proved to be, an "entering wedge" granted our fore-fathers. In the eyes of the Great and General Court, it established the right to allow the petitioners in the west end, a new town and to place the "meeting-house" on the hill.

Now then, with the confines for the parsonage lands well defined, let us again retrace our steps and follow our fathers, as they put the affairs of the parish on a firm and lasting basis; very soon to organize the church, which under leaders well chosen, proved an organization to meet the issues of the two centuries.

—THREE—

MATTERS CONCERNING THE SETTLEMENT OF THE MINISTER

During 1727, (or at least for a part of the year), Mr. Sargent had served the parish as pastor. We have also read that, he was to continue for the following year. At a town meeting on March 12, 1729, we find this record:

> . . . voted to give Mr. Cristoper Sargent for sallery eighty pounds per year for the first fouer years and then to give ninty pounds per year for the next fouer years and after that to give one hundred pounds sper year so long as he shall continue with us in the work of the minstry.

At this time also, a committee was chosen "to erect a pulpit in the meeting house."

In this same meeting, a motion was made "to provide timber for the seats in the meeting house." A decided negative was the answer to this. The vote on the salary question was not immediately agreed upon. Mr. Sargent had a counter proposal. Thus reads the record:

> . . . that the town give me 80 pounds for the first two years. 90 for the next two years and then 100 per year as long as I shall continue with you in the work of the ministry & also thirty cord of wood yearly from the time that I begin to keep house. (Mr. Sargent was married in 1730.) that you give me two hundred pounds in money or labour and materials att the price currant as I shall want ye Towards Bealding to be paid by ye next september com twelve month or other wais if the present circumstances of your town he such as Render it Difficult to you to advance so much toward settlement at present That you pay one hundred of ye afore sd in money at the end of fouer years from this present.

We find this additional proposal indicative not so much of the so-called Yankee shrewdness as the desire on the part of the young minister to seek a living wage. At this time he was twenty five years of age.

. . .but as to the parsonage Land you do in convenant Time, fence in about thirty acres of the best and most conveanant of it and prepare part thereof for mowing and planting and allso that the fence be kept all wais in Repair and that you do make nedfull addittion to my salery as your circumstances will allow & and my necessity calls for it ye yearly sallery to be paid at two payments.

We may say in passing that these proposals were summarily rejected by the voters of the town.

Continual dickerings and adjournments are recorded regarding the much mooted question of salary. Whether it was a question of economy or a revival of the old scores and sores, left by the east and west sections, as to the location of the meetinghouse, or simply the human element of the minister seeking a wage yielding a comfortable living, we know not. Suffice it to state that, the issue drags on even to the season of ordination. Coupled with this problem is the one of securing a grant from the General Court of, additional "province land that Lyeth in This Town," as well the appointment of a committee to petition to the proprietors of the common and undivided land in Haverhill for a piece of land for a parsonage that lies between the meeting house and Spicket River, that was formerly intended in Haverhill Town book for the use of a parsonage. The final arrangements regarding the salary question seem to have been made at an adjourned meeting on April 28, 1729, when the new minister was given:

80 pounds a year, for the first four years and then, 100 a year, long as he shall continue and 10 yearly in lew of parsonage and fire wood and also one hundred pounds Greetis towards settlement to be paid in labour and money and materals toward building by next September come twelve month.

We read that the salary was to be paid "one half att the end of every half yeare.". . . "to begin on the twentieth of March last" (1729). But one pew was to built in the meeting house and that for the minister's family; "the rest to be filled with seats." In a record of about a year later, we detect a further desire on the part of the people to care for then pastor by a vote to spend seventeen shillings for "fethers and Lining for the minister's Cushern."

14

But. the important season in connection with the church itself is approaching. The covenant is to be drawn up and signed by its loyal supporters. The young leader is to receive ordination into the Christian ministry. The First Parish had functioned for a little over two years. Now, the Church, as an organization, is to attend to the spiritual side and even to this day marks the religious life of the organization.

May not this period stand out in the annals of our home institution? Here emerges a power in this early parish, where through tempest and storm; through weather fair and foul; through dickerings and petitions, we may behold a factor playing so important a part in our early New England life. To us here in our own church life there comes the "vision splendid." It is of this old church in its youth substantially founded, built on the hill, ever in the mind and before the eye of a pioneer band of men and women who had braved "the breaking waves" of this rock-bound coast" in order to live; live untrammeled by kings and bishops. Rigid in their views, unmovable in doctrine, sturdy in step. We repeat: they built that they might live, yes, that we may live. No reader of these line; no worshipper at this old shrine of two hundred years standing can do otherwise than stand with bowed head in devotion to the memory of those who did things well.

—FOUR—

THE COVENANT. SIGNERS. ARRANGEMENTS FOR THE ORDINATION. EQUIPMENT FOR THE COMMUNION TABLE; THE ORDINATION. ANCESTRY OF CHRISTOPHER SARGENT

On Sept. 9, 1729, Robert Swan, Henry Bodwell, Joshua Swan, John Gutterson and Lieut. Stephen Barker were chosen a committee "for the ordaining of Mr. Sargent" We are told that Mr. Sargent was settled over the church on Oct. 29, 1729. We read that the day was kept as one of fasting and prayer preparatory to the ordination itself, which came about a week later. We can almost see the good people coming from their homes on the hill and in the dale; along the trail or path, many on horse, more on foot. Let us remember that the town of Salem, N. H., and a good part of Windham, was included in early Methuen. We speak this day of our town covering so many miles in extent, along the Merrimac. But when we consider the stretch of country, from the River north into Windham, and west to Dracut, coupled with the dense growth of the primeval forest, through which the sturdy yeoman must wend his way, we should never complain of our obligations to support an institution in which the very fabric of our New England life is woven.

With the feeling that the devotion evidenced in the deep faith of our forbears may find a response within the breasts of our readers, let us read the covenant subscribed to by twenty one individuals on this 29th day of October 1729 proclaiming a truth never to be lost sight of in after years: moreover, never from life itself.

The covenant:

We whose names are hereunto subscribed, apprehending ourselves called of God to enter into the church state of the Gospel do first of all confess ourselves unworthy of so great privileges and favors, and admire that free and rich grace of His, which triumphs over so great unworthiness and then with an humble reliance on the aids of grace therein promised for them that, in a sense of their inability to do any good thing, do humbly wait on Him for all we are, now thankfully lay hold on His covenant and would choose the things that please him. We declare our serious belief in the Christian religion as contained in the Sacred Scriptures, and with such a view thereof as the confession of our churches has exhibited heartily resolving to conform our lives to the rules of that whole religion as long as we live in this world. We give up ourselves unto the Lord Jehovah, who is the Father, the Son and the Holy Ghost and avouch Him this day to be our God, our Father, our Savior, and our Leader receive Him for our portion forever. We give ourselves to the blessed Jesus, who is the Lord Jehovah, and adhere to Him as the head of His people in the covenant of grace, and rely on Him, as our Prophet, Priest and King, to bring us to eternal glory. We acknowledge our indispensable obligation to glorify our God, in all the duties of a sober, righteous and godly life. And very particularly, in the duties of a church state, as body of people associated for obedience to Him in all ordinances of the Gospel and we depend on His gracious assistance for our faithful discharge of the duties thus incumbent upon us.

We desire and intend, and with dependence on His promise and powerful grace, we engage to walk together as church of the Lord Jesus Christ in the faith and order of the Gospel, so far as we shall have the same revealed to us conscientiously attending the public worship of God, the sacraments of the New Testament, the discipline of His kingdom, and all His Holy institutions in communion one with another, and watchfully avoiding sinful stumbling blocks and contentions as becomes a people whom the Lord has bound up in the bundle of life. At the same time, we do present our offspring with ourselves to the Lord, promising with His help to do our part in the method of a religious education that they may be the Lord's.

And all this we do, flying to the blood of the everlasting covenant, for the pardon of our many errors, and praying that the glorious Lord, who is the great Shepherd, would prepare and strengthen us to every good work to do His will, working in us that which is well pleasing in His sight to whom be glory forever and ever Amen

We have cited this early covenant because we believe it draws the picture of the religious zeal and spiritual energy of our Puritan ancestors. In their new meeting-house, they stand with bowed heads before the living God, speaking the very words of life itself. Set in a frame of gold, the picture never failed to lead them onward and upward. The strong tenets of the early Calvinist church, as expressed in all their vigor in this their creed, became a working faith. In such the old church has grown gray. We shall find the extreme. We shall end the proverbial splitting of the hair, but their devotion never failed. It became our heritage. May it never fail us, and our children's children.

On this day the covenant was "owned" by the following twenty-four men: (We take our spelling directly from the records) Sergeant Steph'n Barker, Jno. Gutterson, Joseph More, Zebed Barker, Tho. Silver, Evans Jones, Tho. Asen, Ben'n Stevens, James Barker, Joseph, Gutterson, Rich. Kelly, Will'm Gutterson, Jho. Messer, Abial Kelley, Jno. Baily, Sam'l Clark, Jona'n Corliss, Isaas Clough, Dan'el Peaslee, James How, Jn'o Typet, Robart Swan.

[1] *Women who signed the covenant: Elizabeth (Lovejoy) Barker, wife of Zebediah; Lydia Barker; Sarah (Lovejoy) Austin, wife of Thomas; Mehitable Barker,; Moriah (Bigsby) Barker, wife of James; Annis (Phelps) Stevens, wife of Benjamin.*

To the reader comes the thought that all the signers are men. Let us state that this fact is evident only at the first meeting.[1] On Nov. 30, following, twenty-seven more consented to the covenant of which number twenty-one were women.

In Mr. Sargent's own words, recorded over his signature in the church book of records we read:

> This was done and at the same time the church called me to the pastors office. In the presence ol' Sam'l Phillips, John Barnard, Joseph Parsons, Pain Winget.

We may state the Rev. Samuel Phillips was the first minister of the South Parish in Andover, where he was ordained on Oct. 17, 1711. John Barnard was minister of the North Parish in Andover and ordained there April 19, 1719. Joseph Parons was minister of the First Church in Bradford, and Pain Winget of the church in West Amesbury, Ma.

At this same meeting (Oct. 28, 1729), arrangements were made for the ordination itself set for Nov. 5, and that the two Churches in Andover, the Church in Haverhill, the First Church in Bradford, Second in Amesbury, and the Second Church in Kittery, send "their ministers, elders and messengers" to constitute the council for this important occasion. That a goodly number of pastors and laymen were responsive to these letters missive, is recorded in an item in the town records where we read:

> On Nov 4 of the same year, the town voted that the committee shall provide for Twenty of thirty ministers and messengers for the ordaining of Mr. Sargent.

In connection with the material equipment of the church let us mention the "vessels" and "cloth" for the communion table in our possession this day; actual reminders of two hundred years since. The records thus read:

> The Communion Table of this Church furnished as follows: Mr. Nath'll Penslee of Haverhill gave a flaggon pr. 3-0-0. Mr. Osgood of Andover gave another flaggon pr. 3-0-0.. Mrs. Mary Sargeant of Amesbury gave at Table Cloth pr. 2-10-0. Andover old Chh gave three Tankards. Methuen Chh contributed 3-15-0 to purchas a. Napkin 0-17-6 a Christianing bason & two

Dishes 1-17-6 a Chh Book 0-6-9 a Tankard 0-10-0. Total 3-11-9 and the Remaining 0-3-0 to ye Decon for his trouble in procuring them.

May we state that the "Andover old church," is the present Unitarian Church in North Andover. At that time, 1730, it was strictly orthodox and the oldest in the Andover township. Organized in 1645 it was six years older than the present Old South Church. We quote a letter of the Rev. Frank R. Shipman to Mrs. Woodbury, which thus reads:

the Rev. John Barnard's 'Journal' which was in effect the North Church Records during his pastorate, speaks of the purchase of three silver tankards under date 19 May 1728. A year later 5 May 1729 some plates were bought - to go with the tankards apparently. Still a year later occurs the entry which you want. "At a Church Meeting May 4, 1730. "Voted, that Deacon Osgood, present ye Church of Methuen the 3 pewter tankards, (which the Church has no occasion for) in the name of ye Church.

Mr. Shipman adds that he finds no record about such action in connection with the South Church and no further items as to the North Church. These are believed to be the vessels now so carefully preserved in our church.

As to the "Table Cloth" mentioned above, may we say that such is still in a wonderful state of preservation; a fine homespun specimen of linen, measuring three feet eight and one half inches by seven feet four inches. Across the face of this is carefully embroidered in yellow silk these words: "A Gift of Mistris Mary Sergeant to the Church of Methuen, 1729." During the coming observance of the Two Hundredth Anniversary, we shall endeavor to use those utensils at the out-of-doors communion service to be held by the grave of the Rev. Christopher Sargent. Also that from the "Sargent-Record" by Edwin Everett Sargent of St. Johnsbury, Vt. we find "Mistris Mary" to be a second-cousin of Christopher Sargent and a year younger.

The committee named above, Robert Swan, Stephen Barker and John Gutterson, was delegated "to send out the letters in the name of the Ch.-" No such important event on the calendar of our church life this day, has ever been better arranged, than was this of two centuries ago. From the records, so carefully kept by the pastor, Mr. Sargent and preserved during these many years, we have the program of the exercises of ordination. The original records are fast fading on pages yellow with age. We are fortunate to preserve these for coming generations. The opening prayer was by the Rev. John Brown of Haverhill, where he had been ordained on May 13, 1719. The Sermon for ordination was preached, by Rev. John Rogers of the First Church in Ipswich. He was the son of John Rogers, President of Harvard College; a man of wide learning, whose influence was a factor throughout the region. His text was chosen from 2 Cor. 3,5. The charge to the young pastor was given by the Rev. Samuel Phillips of the South Church in Andover. This strong leader in the Andover church held a useful ministry in that town for sixty years. Ordained in 1711, with the experience of eighteen years, we feel certain that from him came the best of advice for our Mr. Sargent. From this neighbor in the ministry, he received the right-hand of fellowship. The closing prayer was offered by Rev. Joseph Parsons, a visiting clergyman, who at that time, was preaching in Haverhill, as a supply or possibly a candidate for the church in that town. The records tell us that, "they four laid on hands"; thus began the long pastorate of the first leader of our home church.

Before closing this chapter and entering upon the next, which may relate some of the activities of the pastorate itself, it seems fitting to devote a bit of space allowing us to look into the ancestry and equipment, of this young man for the important work to continue for three generations. He, who was shepherd to our fathers for fifty four years, and for seven years, lived among them as their aged friend and counselor, was born in Amesbury Aug. 4, 1704. He was the great grandson of William Sargent. As clearly as we can discern, this ancestor was living in Agawam (now Ipswich), in 1633; later moving to Salisbury New Town, now Amesbury and Merrimac in 1655, where he died in 1675. From his will duly "Entered and Recorded in ye County record for Norfolk and inventory as appraised, he left an estate valued 191 pounds." Of his nine children, the third child Thomas, the grandfather of Christopher, was born in Salisbury; a farmer, holder of many public offices, a lieutenant in the local militia. His son, the father of our young minister was born in Amesbury, Nov. 15, 1676. On Dec. 17, 1702, he married Mary Stevens, also of Amesbury. He was a farmer and held offices in Amesbury. Five children were born to them. The oldest, Christopher, appeared to represent the solid traits and character of the early settler. And what about the early settlers? We must never forget that the ancestry of our day and generation were not mere sea-rovers. They were not traders, attracted by the prospect of inordinate profits. They were not paupers, seeking better economic conditions. On the other hand, they represented the best of the English nation. Many were graduates of the English universities.

From this class of men and women settling in a new land; in homes carved from the very depths of these primeval forests, was developed the Yankee. He, who cherished his home, fostered his school and revered his God. Christopher Sargent was a graduate of Harvard College in the class of 1725. Somehow these words ring deep and loud. That a boy brought up in a typical New England family, had graduated from college and fitted himself for pastoral work at the age of twenty five years. The reader might ask to his theological training and education. The answer is simple. The puritan home read its Bible, more than that, it studied the good Book. It had no competitor in the line of secular reading. We know that the young leader had heard matters theological, discussed daily, in his own home. We feel certain that, at an early age he could participate in these discussions.

Above, we have read of the bargaining carried on ,as regards his salary. From the story, we might imagine that he was representative of the typical Yankee shrewdness. To the world, this trait has ever been coupled with those named. This type generally, (perhaps we should say quite often), secures what it seeks. We believe Mr. Sargent did.

It was such an equipment, inherent and developed, that made the young leader what he was. More than that, it made the church what it was, and what it became. An institution built upon the lasting rocks of faith, hope, and love.

That this sketch may bear out this assertion, is the hope of the writer.

—FIVE—

CHURCH PROBLEMS, WITHIN. AND WITHOUT. FORMATION OF THE NORTH-PARISH CHURCH. THE NEW TOWN SALEM, N. H.

The church and parish are now real factors in the life of the new town. For several decades, they are the very guide of life. The student of history reads of the New England theocracy. Some writers have endeavored to nullify the term. But it existed. We are to see this fact as we unfold the pages, written large in local affairs. Many a New England town has had its minister who ruled; and he ruled with at strong arm. We are not saying that Mr. Sargent so lived, and yet his influence as leader of the vigorous institution now founded, was a strong one. Let this chapter tell us of some of his trials; of his problems. Church problems galore were in evidence. We may illustrate later. Cases of discipline, and there were many, were immediately considered. Public scandal of any kind, called for summary expulsion from the church; from Full Communion, as the records read. Persons belonging to a church in other towns, but not worshipping here, if this be their place of residence, "must seek their letters of dismission, so as to unite with us in convenient time or be deprived of worship with us." Some were behind in payment of dues to support the sacrament. They were ordered to pay their arrears, "before the next sacrament," or "be suspended from communion until it be paid." On Nov. 30, 1732, we read that "each member pay 1 pound 3 pence to defray Communion Charge for ye commg year and to make up past arrears." At this distance, it might appear that a gradual withdrawal from the church would solve the question. But, we must not forget the "New England conscience." The guiding

22

element in their lives was the spiritual. There were exceptions, but until the last quarter of the century, such were in the minority. Cases of discipline were regular incidents. Profanity was evidently an common a trait in those days as in later years. All such cases were immediately reported to the church. Public acknowledgment was demanded; sometimes before the committee delegated to investigate the charges, more often before the congregation as a whole assembled in the "meeting house." Absence from the communion service was a reprehensible act. Such an offender was immediately ordered to report at the next "Church meeting," with explanations for his short comings.

Illustrative of the controlling power of the religious in the life of the day, let us cite the following case taken directly from the records:

July ye 5th 1733, at a Ch Meeting to hear the Difference between Deacon How & Thomas Silver a charge being made against Sd Silver of falsehood in Denying an agreement between them concerning ye lands the Ch considering yt matter as it then appeared looked upon it as not cognizable by ye Ch being a matter of civil concern yt belonged more properly to ye law to determine but at the same time a charge being made against sd Silver of profane and sinful language In saying yt How was a cursed deceitful fellow as goes upon ye earth with him. yt he was the Devilishest cursed fellow yt ever G. made, or in words to this purpose (as attested by Stephen Barker Sr. Wm Cross) which charge was acknowledged by sd Silver who professed his sorrow & repentance for his sinful passion and language and asked forgiveness of ye Ch. and of How in particular wh. was accordingly granted & accepted by a vote of ye Ch-.

However, as is quite often with public apologies, the case again appeared. For on the following Oct. 25 we again read that:

. . . at a Ch. meeting after settling the Deacon's act for the year past The case of Thomas Silver being again considered it appeared by evedence yt the sd Silver had charged Deacon How with being a cursed lyer or sd he lived cursedly if he said he had ever made any agreement under the hands & seels of the parties appearing. It was voted yt sd Silver be suspended from Ch. Communion with us till he make publick acknowledgment of its being a false & profane & sinful charge or give Christian Satisfaction.

Indicative of the "follow up" policy, as regards the discipline of the church, let us add that the case in hand hung over or rather remained unsettled for many months. Just a year later we read:

> . . .at a Ch. meeting Ch again took into consideration the case of Thomas Silver who rs under suspention for calling Deacon how a Cursed Lyer etc. &c. and he making no reasonable satisfaction but continuing Impenetant & obstinate ye Ch voted unanimously to continue his suspention and to administer a word of admonition to him publiekly for his sin & obstrnacy therein.

A careful reading of the records would indicate that Silver remained "obstinate," until July 2, 1740, when "making a satisfactory acknowledgement for his offence for which he had been suspended was again restored to Com."

All the above was church discipline. Our puritan ancestry certainly kept in touch with all breaches of the moral law. If a man was fit to "own the covenant," and be taken into "full communion," he was fit to be a peace loving citizen. We may oft wonder at the dividing line between the civil and divine law. Let us not forget that the church was a living organism. It taught a religion for Monday, as well as for Sunday.

Let us now turn from the parishioner to pastor. Church disturbances were not confined to the flock at large. At times, disturbances were not confined to the flock at large. At times the leader himself, became the object of attack. While Mr. Sargent was a stern and rigid teacher and expounder of the Old Testament, there were members of his flock, who in their own lines thought out and discussed theological views. Here we read from the report of a church meeting of May 4, 1743:

> . . . .at a church meeting ye church took into consideration the case of Abraham Adams who was charged with declaiming publickly in ye face of ye Congregation on Febr. ye 13th last year that Mr. Sargent had been mocking God that Day & leading souls down to Hell he owned and intended justified. there upon ye ch voted (1) that he had not made out his charge in yr opinion (2) that the he might think himself obliged in conscience to say wt he did yet wc look upon it. disorderly & a thing of ill tendancy to express himself in such a manner at such a time upon no better

ground (3) that henceforth ye Ch look upon him unfit for Communion with them at ye Lord's Table in this present. frame". "N. B. ye Defence sd Adams made for himself in support of his Charge seaured to be in substance this: that sd Sergeant his pastor had been defective in ye private duties of his ministry that he had not given him such account of his experiences as to make him believe he was a converted man & therefore could be no minister of J. X. & so could do nothing but lead souls to Hell. & then demanded an account of his experiences before ye Ch. that he had refused to let such ministers preach in his pulpit as himself desined & therefore was lighting against God that he preached up a covenant of work without showing it the way to X (and this asserted without producing any particular passage in any sermon for proof) that he had explained ye natural man in a wrong sence in ye afternoon of ye Sabbath when he made ye above declaration against him which was done between meetings. and that wt he had thus declared against his minister on sd day he was satisfied was for ye glory of God because he had kept yo preceeding day as a Day of fasting & prayer for Direction that if wt he had designed to say was for ye Glory of God he might, speak not that his mouth might be stopped.

Six years afterward, Adams sent in his confession and was received back into the church.

Would that we had the space to tell of a charge brought against the minister in 1754. It startles us to read that men from the parish were able to discuss such abstruse subjects. In one particular case, an impromptu court was held. Rev. Joseph Parsons from Haverhill sat as Moderator. Mr. Sargent was invariably able to defend his doctrines; and yet, such occurrences meant coming disturbances in the life of the parish and church.

We have repeatedly referred to the extent of the township as a whole. Its northern and western boundaries were so far distant from the center, which we may describe as the region adjacent to the meeting-house on the Hill, that men were naturally to petition for relief either in the "rate" levied upon them or (as we shall now see), by asking for a church of their own.

The first move of this nature came on March 13, 1734, when a petition was presented by the residents of the north section, that they be set off a parish by themselves in order, "to maintain the publick worship of God." As in the days of a decade past, the request was refused. The First Parish felt as did the town of

Haverhill, to lose a part of their territory, would result only in a diminution of taxes. It took several requests to bring about the desired lands. It was a case of "try and try again." Eventually the petition was granted, and the town of Salem, New Hampshire resulted. But it came not easily. On Oct. 22, 1734, we read that it was voted:

> . . . to add teen pounds more to the minister Rate the next year in answer to a petition of Spicket Hill pepell for sum ease in their corst in Hiering a minster to preach amongst them four months in the winter season the next winter if they hier one four month.

We cite these details merely to tell of the persistence of the northern section in securing the separation from the mother church; as well to indicate the effort of the latter to hold the church together; also to bring out still another evidence of men's loyalty to their religious vows.

From the earliest records in the town of Salem, N. H., we learn of a petition presented by Henry Sanders and associates, addressed to the Great and General Court or Assembly, for the province of Massachusetts Bay, to call the first parish meeting with a desire that, "the inhabitants qualified to vote in parish affairs, do meet at the house of Daniel Peaslee, on Thursday the 16th day of Jan." This was in 1735-6.

The purpose was to arrange for the election of parish officers to stand, until the March meeting; to pay a Mr. Greenleaf for, "preaching with us this winter;" to see if, "ye parish will lay out a burying ground."

We find no details of this informal meeting, but we do read of a meeting on January 24, at which a full board of town officers was chosen and a regular committee appointed, to "warn parish meetings;" "to lay out a burying place;" and also voted "to raise 45 pounds for support of ye ministry." Repeated petitions to the town of Haverhill for land for a parsonage, resulted in the proprietors of that town allowing the north parish fifty acres for a parsonage and the same number for their first ordained minister, "to encourage him to settle amongst them".

These lands lay "by the Spicket," west of the road, now leading from Salem Center up over Spicket Hill. The first meeting-house was built in the late fall of 1738. The church as distinct from the parish was organized in Jan. 1740. This first house of worship stood on, what we now know, as the common at the center. The original frame was used in the construction of the town hall, now standing a few rods east of the original site. Behind by the river can be seen the old "burying ground." The first minister was Mr. Abner Bailey, called Nov. 13, 1739, at a salary of one hundred forty pounds in bills of credit, according as bills of credit are payable at this time.

We trust the reader has not tired of these details. Inside disturbances, as well as problems from without, so stand out in the early years of our old parish, that we have thus grouped them in this chapter. The second half of this century is to bring about even more important matters, which we shall defer to another chapter. A strong leader of an equally rugged people, is to face issues greater than those of the region itself.

– SIX –

LIBERALISM. THE SECOND PARISH. "SEPARATISTS". RESIGNATION OF CHRISTOPHER SARGENT

The middle of the eighteenth century is to find our western world continually disturbed. The prolonged struggles between the great powers of the old world in the east are to be trans-ferred to our shores. The territory north, south, and west of this early settled region, was steadily occupied by those mighty powers all intent on securing what had been seized by an adver-sary. English, Dutch, and Spanish settlements south and west were thwarted by the then powerful France in the north and north-west. We cannot enter in detail at this time to the move-ments of these nations. But we must merely state that little New England, Massachusetts Bay Colony, the frontier-town, here and there, were to feel more than a passing interest in the new influences brought to bear upon the life of a growing nation. We have stated in the previous chapter that Mr. Sargent's orthodoxy was frequently questioned.

A feeling of religious unrest was sweeping through the country. Other sects were preaching new doctrines. The liberal views of French idolatry attending the coming Revolution in this country exerted an influence, which our own church was to experience. Of these changing views, with resulting conditions, we shall speak as the occasion requires. To us with the years of progress behind, they may appear trivial; to our father they were far otherwise. Perhaps the organization of a second parish out of the very vitals of the First, was as disturbing as any question facing them. On the 9th of April, 1766, in response to a petition from citizens in the west part, the town voted "to poll off those persons with their inheritance whose names are given." Then follow the names of sixty citizens living west of the Spicket. In the list appears the name of one woman: "Widow Mary Cross."

The inception of this second parish seems to have arisen from the influence of several religious sects taking root among the families of this scattered region. It was the oldest part of the town, (probably). Men in that section possibly were not so closely held by the ties of the old parish in the east section. The Calvinist had his troubles along the lines of predestination and free will. Mr. Sargent's troubles grew out of discussions along these lines. The Baptist was making his influence felt. At this time, a church of this denomination existed in Haverhill. The would-be "separatists" were bound to persevere and to succeed. The "polling off" of the list above mentioned was a reality. They constructed a small church building a short distance from Spicket Falls. In an itinerary described by a Rev. William Bently in 1787-1799, (From the records of the Topsfield Historical Society, we find these words: let us state that they follow his description of the region about Spicket Falls,) "We left the Meeting House & continued our route eastward, after having been informed that we left the Meeting House of the Separat-

28

ists, half a mile on our left to the west when we were at the Falls." From this description, as well the generally accepted statements of the older residents of the town, we believe this church stood on what is known as the Leonard Wheeler farm. This day we may know it even better as that of the late Stephen D. Crowell on Pelham Street. One of our oldest inhabitants speaks of a depression in the land just west of the house, where was supposed to stand the foundation wall of the church. Scattered records, carefully preserved and now in possession of the writer, tell us that on June 6, 1787:

> . . . the parish voted to give up their promiscuous parish, in case the town of Methuen would set off a competency of Poles and Estates to the parishes acceptance in the western part of Methuen and in case the town of Dracut also would set off competency of poles and estate in the easterly part of their town to this parishes acceptance to make one parish.

A movement was also started to purchase the farm of Eliphaz Chapman an early pastor of the second parish, for a parsonage, in the west-part of the town. Finally after many dickerings it would appear that the parish was grouped around a new church center. Joined with east Dracut, Pelham and the adjoining part of Salem, N.H. it established a meeting-house on what we know as Williams Hill. The vote on March 30, 1789 was to

> . . . raise 75 Poinds to support gospel present year to join with Pelham to have gospel Minister to hire Preaching, Draw money out of Treasury to pay candidates.

The parish had a struggling existence. Continual differences arose with the First Parish regarding rates. Not recognizing the need of harmony, each antagonized the other. The names of Osgood, Barker, Gutterson, Pettingill, Richardson, occur often in connection with this second church. In about the year 1778 a small Baptist society existed in the west part. Their small crudely built church, (as Bently tells us in the diary quoted above,) "is at some distance on the extreme part of the Town toward Dracut and is unfinished & without a Teacher." Tradition tells us this, was south of our present Elmwood cemetery, on the west side of the road, near Bartlett's Brook.

We speak of these efforts to establish other centers of worship simply to keep before our minds the fact that the old first church still "carries on." The second parish was eventually received back unto the fold. Let us retrace our steps to our meeting-house on the hill and cull from the records before us.

The question of "that part of the service called singing," was for some time an issue unsettled. That such was a form of levity appears to have been the cause. The first settlement of this item seems to have been in 1782, when it was voted at the Parish Meeting that they "read the Psalm & choose Joseph Morss, Deacon Jno. Harris, Samuel Huse, Jacob Mirick & Capt. Stephen Webster is Quoixmasters."

Included in the laws of the New England towns was one forbidding the cutting of white pine trees of the diameter of twenty inches or upwards, twelve inches from the ground on any but private land. Whether the officials of the parish were fearful of Mr. Sargent's choice of firewood or because of the desire to conserve the growing timber, we know not; it may have been the one desire to provide for the aged pastor. At any rate there was an article in the warrant for a meeting in 1782, "to see if the parish will Hall Ten Cords of wood for the Rev. Mr. Sargent to prevent his cutting on the parsonage the year ensuing". The vote was passed "to procure wood on the Parish Cost."

We must note that now in the seventies Mr. Sargent has reached an age when he must lay down the reins and another take up the work of his many years. In 1778,

> ... In answer to a petition of a Number of Inhabitants to see if Parish will take into Consideration Certain proposals made by the Rev. Mr. Christopher Sargent some time in the year 1778, relative to his leaving the desk and act as they shall think best.

—SEVEN—

The settlement of the question regarding the retirement of the aged pastor on a stipulated salary and the engagement of his successor seem to have been long drawn out problems. A Mr. Jacob Wood was engaged "for the remainder of the half-year." In fact, for some months to come, we find Mr. Wood the regular "supply." In Feb. 1783, an interesting vote was passed to give Mr. Sargent, one hundred pounds with an exemption of half his public taxes, during his natural life, providing he claims no more salary and asks no further use of the parsonage. A copy of this "discharge" follows:

Methuen Feby 10th, 1783. In Consideration of the Sum of One Hundred pounds. My this day granted to me the Subscriber by the First Parish in sd Town & Relinquishing one half of my estate from publick Taxes during my natural life I do hereby discharge myself of any claim to my Salary or any part thereof for the Futher on account of my being the gospel Minister of sd Parish & do also Relinquish my right in the Parsonage Lands in sd Parish & do here signifie that I will by no means obstruct the settlement of another gospel minister in sd Parish in a regular manner & upon such settlement will relinquish the pastoral office if desired. So wishing you divine Directions in such an Important concern and that you may be given again happily settled in peace under the care of a godly faithful minister of Jesus Christ, which is the hearty prayer of your loving pastor——Christopher Sargent.

In June 1783 a Mr. Bell was engaged. to preach, "until further notice." On Feb. 12, 1784, the parish voted that Mr. Jacob Wood "is allowed one hundred pounds as a settlement," or that "the parish will procure him convenient Parsonage Buildings which he pleaseth." This vote had followed one of the church on Jan. 15, "by a great majority to give Mr. Jacob Wood a call." We further read that he, "afterward gave his answer in ye Negative." On March 23, Jno. Huse is allowed two pounds and nine pence, for boarding Mr. Bell and his horse six weeks, and Mr. Wood and horse seventeen weeks.

We are in a period when the laxity in settling a pastor is bringing about a disturbing condition. A small minority in the parish appear to have been opposed to "calling" Mr. Wood. This indifference continued several years. Above we have spoken of the overturn in the religious world. The acts of the northern and western sections of the town now find an echo from the south when in 1784 a petition comes from, "the southerly part of the town to see if the parish will release any part of their minister rate." Such petition was rejected. This was in June; in August of the same year came another, to see if like privileges will be granted to those in "the westerly part of said town." The action taken is thus recorded:

Then took into consideration the proposals made by the assessors & a number of the inhabitants in westerly part of the Parish who profess to be Baptist, which was that the whole dispute as to their paying or not paying their minister Tax be left tin a committee of three indifferent men of the party, if they agree well, if not, they to choose two indifferent men, if they agree well if not they (viz) the two men to choose the third and they to settle the whole matter." James Ingalls, Peter Marston and Jno Huse were the committee chosen. The assessors were directed to notify the parties and prefix a time and place of meeting.

In Sept. of this same year (1784) a meeting was called "to see whether the said Parish will settle with Revd Mr. Sargent or whether the parish will let the action go to court that Mr. Sargent hath commenced against said parish." At this distance, a pitiful situation appears imminent. Here is the good old pastor who has served his people three generations now, in his eighty-first year threatening to sue for his one hundred pounds, voted him by his parish, as he laid down his work, to live in retirement during the few remaining years of his life. A committee was chosen to consult with Mr. Sargent. Said committee reported, and the vote was passed that they do not, "comply with the proposals made by Mr. Sargent." A short time later, a new committee of two men was chosen, to try to bring about an arrangement. When presented, this vote was taken:

> ... that the Rev. Mr. Sargent's sallery which is not recipted for be made good according to the Scale, that the corn which is due be stated at 4p per bushl and that the other arreers be paid with interest from the time they were due and that the Treasury be directed to give him a Note upon Interest from the whole Sum due together- with the cost df the writ and Service, and likewise Voted that the Treasury be directed to gather the Money and pay it as soon as possible.

A committee of three was chosen, "for carrying the afore sd Vote in to execution if complyed with."

In Nov. of this same year, it was voted to engage a Mr. Allen for three months; also that if any candidate was not paid within three months from his first appearance, the treasurer was to give him a note on the parish with interest.

In the following year, a number of individuals appear asking abatement on their "minister-tax." In 1785, it was voted "not to engage Mr. Allen any longer." A vote was taken to sell the parsonage and then, immediately rescinded, and voted to lay out, "12 or 15 acre of ye east end of ye parsonage. to clear ye land & wall ye same. ye Lumber thereon standing to be sold to ye highest bidder to pay ye cost."

The vote to release Mr. Allen is reconsidered, and a vote taken "to hire him for three months." Parish meetings were called easily and often in those days. Here is one for June 6, 1785, with the one article, "to see what ye parish will act Respecting ye Meeting-house windows being broke & act thereon as they Shall think proper." The reader detects evidence of the gang rowdy, even at that time, for here as the result of the above:

> ... voted of ye assessors be & are hereby impowered & directed to use their best Endeavors to find out who were ye persons conserned in breaking is Meeting house Windows & to Prosecute ye same to Final issue being in a Just account of ye Cost at a futer parish meeting for allowance.

At this time, a Mr. Cram is recorded as the temporary preacher. In all probability, he was another of a number of candidates. In Sept. 1785, he is engaged for six weeks longer. Also it was voted, "to let the Parsonage Pew to the highest bidder." In March of the next year, we find the name of a Mr. Bradford as candidate. In Sept. 1785, there was a vote to unite with the Second Parish in hiring the minister, each parish paying in proportion to the minister rates of that parish.

To the reader there doubtless comes the thought that, the old church is passing through a season of depression. We must remember, that these are days following the Revolutionary War, when as is the case after any upheaval, times are "hard." The country has been drained of men and means. A readjustment is needed, even as we have found after the World War. As we have intimated above, other denominations had sprung up in these parts. Other churches in this town acted in more or less competition, especially the little second parish, which must necessarily have been a thorn in the side of the old parish.

However, affairs soon come back to "normalcy." The work of the past half century has been built upon a lasting basis. The church emerges from its lethargy and the influence anew is brought into the affairs of the town.

—EIGHT—

The second minister Rev. Simon Finley Williams. His troubles.
Adoption of the Cambridge Platform.

On July 20, 1786, "At a Ch. meeting ye Brethren of ye church unanimously Gave Mr. Symon Willams a call to ye Work of ye ministry in this Place." In the parish records, to concur with the action of the church in calling a muster, the article in the warrant read as follows: "To see if ye Parish will vote to hire Mr. Williams to supply ye desk after his engagement is up, for which he now supplies sd desk." It was voted, "to hire Mr. Williams longer," a month later, a second parish meeting was called; a special meeting with the one article in which it was voted "to engage Mr. Williams three months longer to preach upon probation." Such act evinces an element unwilling to allow peace and harmony in the church and parish. It is, furthermore, an argument against the two organizations. More and more, even this day, is the value of incorporation becoming evident.

Rev. Simon Finley Williams was the son of Rev. Simon Williams, who was born in Trim, county of Meath, province of Leicester, Ireland, Feb. 19, 1729. The father was highly educated in the English schools and colleges. He came to this country first, as a teacher; to gain a touch of American education, he took a course at the College of New Jersey, Princeton, where he was graduated in 1763. He had nine children; the sixth, was Simon Finley, born in Princeton, New Jersey, July 23, 1764. He married Mary Gregg, daughter of Capt. David Gregg of Windham, N.H. He was graduated from Dartmouth College in 1785. He was ordained pastor of the First Church in Methuen on Dec. 13, 1786; discharged Aug. 16, 1791. His mind became unsettled. He had trouble with his church in Methuen. In Morrison's *History of Windham,* we read that the last hymn given his choir was the 120th Psalm of Dr. Watts; one stanza of which was:

> *"Oh, might I fly to change my place*
> *How would I choose to dwell*
> *In some wide, lonesome wilderness,*
> *AND LEAVE THESE GATES OF HELL.*

Quoting further from Morrison, we find that "he was installed in Meredith, N.H. Nov. 28, 1792; had troubles in church and home. He abandoned his family; was dismissed from his church March 2., 1797, and excommunicated Aug. 28, 1798. The story is that he shipped as chaplain on a frigate and sailed to the East Indies. He was to deliver a Fourth of July ovation in 1802, but died on the 3rd and was buried at sea; but mystery has overhung over his end. His widow supposed him dead and married again, to John Anderson of Windham. Many years afterwards,

35

a stranger appeared in town; he seemed to know Windham history, especially all connected with the Williams family. He visited many Windham families and spent considerable time with Mrs. Anderson. But her lips were ever-sealed, to her dying day, she would never throw any light on the stranger's visit. She died in Londonderry. Many said that this stranger was the Rev. Simon Finley Williams. He had four children.

Coincident with the ordination of Mr. Williams, was the adoption by the church, of the so-called, Cambridge Platform. We take the words directly from the records of the church as follows:

Nov. 2, 1786 we ye Brethren of this Ch. having through ye kind interposition of providence a smiling prospect of resettling in gospel order with a Pastr of our own chusing & desirious to do everything in our Power within Ye Sphere of Christian Duty to lay a solid foundation to subsist in Peace, harmony and Christian love and to revive in our minds a sence of our obligation in particular to watch over one another in faith and love according to ye Tenure & Spirit of our mutual covenant & engagement would upon ye Present occasion vote first our acknowledgment to each other of our sence of ye important duty of Keeping up Ch discipline with Prudence and in ye Spirit of it as ye Gospel directs Sencible yt heretofore we have been too deficient in ye discharge of this Duty as in all others which may have operated as matter of stumbling to some of our Brethren. 2ndly In order yt we may be united in ye mode of Ch discipline we adopt Cambridge Platform (so-called) in ye substance of it as a Rule upon his head. 3rdly That in a resettled state to wh we are hasting with ye aid of our Pastr & ye assistance of Divine Grace we will endeavor a consciencious regard to ye Duty of watching over one another in a Spirit of meekness & Charity. hereby to preserve ye purity of ye Ch in a consistance with ye exercise of Christian Charity.

An interesting vote also taken at this same meeting was that "those who were formerly members of this Ch & have gone to ye Second Ch. in this Town have leave to return to us if they please."

Let us again refer to the "Bentley Dairy" quoted above in Chap. 6:

> Rev. Sargent was succeeded by a Mr. Williams, son of Revd. Williams of Windham, not far from this place, for whom a Manse was built upon the glebe, not far from the Meeting House. Mr. Williams soon left his charge from some civil dispute, & is since settled at Meredith. The dispute began about a wood lot of the Parsonage & a challenge from the pulpit at a weekly Lecture, which one of the Parishioners accepted.

We cannot but feel that, matters spiritual are still in a disturbed condition. Between the lines, we can read that the church and parish are not in true accord. Mr. Williams surely did not bring about the needed adjustment. The interim following the discharge of Mr. Williams was even longer than that following Mr. Sargent before the successor was chosen. With the expressed determination of the people to move slowly and the discordant note often expressed in church affairs, we cannot expect things otherwise. An interval of a little more than four years followed. In 1792, the church extended a call to Mr. Solomon Spalding. In this, the parish refused to concur; this after a divided vote and several "reconsiderations." Candidates were "heard" for three years.

—NINE—

THE THIRD MINISTER REV. HUMPHREY CLARKE PERLEY. THE "FIRST CHURCH OF CHRIST". CONFESSION OF FAITH. MISSIONS AND CALVINISM STRENGTHENED BY THE NEW ANDOVER THEOLOGICAL SEMINARY.

On July 6, 1795, a unanimous call was extended Mr. Humphrey Clark Perley, a native of Boxford. On July 11, the matter was referred to the parish for concurrence. Adjournments and reconsiderations followed. An element in the parish, though in the minority, seemed to block any decision. Whether the question of economy, penury, or prejudice entered into the issue, the reader must decide for himself. We can imagine that even after an agreement was brought about between church and parish, there was still the difficulty to arrange the details. That there were such, and several as well, may be inferred from the report of the committee which follows, taken verbatim from the records; also the reply of Mr. Perley, which may provoke a bit of interest. First the report of the committee chosen to "engage" Mr. Perley:

> 1st the Sum of eighty pounds in money shall be paid him yearly. 2dly that he shall have the sole use of the parsonage (except as is hereafter contained) with the Building Now on the same which shall be kept in good Repair By the parish. 3dly the parish shall procure him twelve cords of hard wood and four cords of pine wood corded at his door yearly and also post can be cut what fencing still is necessary to make and maintain the Necessary wood finer on the parsonage, amendment, at the discretion of the assessors then in Being. In consideration of the sd Perley Relinquishing all Right of cutting off or any way disposing of the timber or wood on the sd Parsonage farm. 4thly the Stipend have voted sd Perley as a support provided he shall settle with them in the gospel ministry shall commence at the time of his giving his answer and shall continue to be paid annually so long as he shall continue with the parish and faithfully carry on the work and Discharge the Duties of a gospel minister. (Short intervals of sickness excepted as all men are subject to disorder.)

In passing let us state that this parsonage "building;" referred to a few lines above and mentioned by Mr. Bentley, was built for Mr. Williams, across the road from the "burying ground" on the "Hill." This was on the sixty acres, granted by "our fathers, in times past, voted and granted for a parsonage." In the *Manual of the Church* adopted in 1875, we read that "it is still standing in good state of preservation." Today it stands, converted into a barn connected with what is known as the Thomas Barstow house; now the home of Mr. Waldemar L. Sjostrom, on the comer of Berkeley and Arlington streets. This was the first "parsonage building" owned by the parish.

Now let us read the reply of Mr. Perley, to the call received from the committee; it is transcribed directly as written:

> Revd. Humphrey Clark Perly   ANSWER
>
> Methuen Oct. 17-1795
>
> Having from time since received an invitation from the first church of Christ & parish in this place, to settle with them in the gospel ministry——I have taken the matter under serious consideration, and that I might be

directed in duty, have asked council of G. & man—And upon mature deliberation- I find there are some things which militate against my complying with the request. But yet the argument in favor of my settling with you appear to be more numerous & weighty, and urge it upon me as an indispensable duty. I therefore give my answer in the affirmative, but being sensible of my insufficiency for these things, & that we have the in- estimable treasure of the Gospel in earthen vessels, that the excellency of the power may be of G. I beseech you my fathers, brothers and friends, to pray the great head of the Church, that I may be enriched with grace, and thoroughly furnished unto every good work. That I may come forth unto you in the fulness of the blessing of the gospel of C. and be made instrument in the hands of G. of saving so alive—that we may live together on earth and Enish our course with joy, & finally all be received to dwell with God forever.

Hump C. Perley   ANSWER

This was read Oct. 18, 1795 by the Rev. John Kelley, (Mr. Kelley was minister at Hampstead, N. H.,)

Agreeable to the desire of the first ch in Methuen- The Ecclesiastical council met & ordained Humphrey Clark Perley to the pastoral office of the first ch In Methuen; He being first voted in as a member. The Rev. Jonathan Allen of Bradford the introductory Prayer—The Revd. Stephen Peabody (of Atkinson, N. H.) preached the sermon—The Revd Jonathan French at Andover made the consecrating prayer—The Revd. William Symms of Andover gave the charge- The Rev. Phineas Adams of Haverhill gave the right hand of fellowship—& The Revd. Peter Eaton of Boxford made the concluding Prayer. The Above said ordination was December 2d, 1. Mr. Perley was born in Boxford, Mass. December 24, 1761. He was a graduate of Dartmouth in the class of 1791. At the age of thirty-two he assumes the pastorate of this church. During his connection with the parish continuing for twenty years, he had more or less a disturbing experience. The many new phases of the work within and the attacks from without could not but be disturbing to a young man called to a church embedded in the very depths of Calvinism. Illustrative of the rigid Trinitarianism holding the old church to the faith of its founders, let us quote the Confession of Faith accepted by the first church of Christ in Methuen May 7, 1797.

(Notice the term "First Church of Christ" now applied to our old institution).

We believe in one God existing in three distinct persons equal in power & glory infinite self-existent, independent, unchangeable, eternal.

We believe man was made at first in the moral image of God & by the transgression of Adam human nature lost its original rectitude.

We believe Christ the second person in the Godhead is equal with the Father also Mediator and Saviour of men.

We believe the holy spirit, the third person in the Godhead is the Sanctifier and comforter.

We believe man since the fall while in a state of nature is destitute of holiness or true love for God.

We believe this life is man's probationary state.

We believe regeneration is necessary to the salvation of sinners.

We believe the scriptures called the word of God were written by the pen of divine inspiration and contain the only rule of faith and practice for sinful man.

We believe after death will be the judgment when all will be rewarded according to the deeds done in the body & that the finally impenitent will go away into everlasting punishment and the righteous into life eternal.

–TEN–

A SECOND MEETING HOUSE RISES ON THE SITE OF THE FIRST. THE SECOND PARISH HAS ITS PROBLEMS. THE "HALF-WAY COVENANT"

The erection of a new church is ever a milestone on the road of a religious life. The old "meeting house" had stood with open doors since 1728. Plainly constructed, unpainted it stood a stern appearing home on the brow of the Hill. Forty feet long, thirty five feet wide and twenty feet stud; unplastered, no stove, no organ, no bell; one pew, and that for the minister's family; benches for the people. Surely, after a period of sixty-eight years, the parish needed a new house of worship.

A committee of twelve was chosen, on ways and means, for the construction of the new building to "set on the site of the old meeting house." It was to be "fifty eight feet in length and forty two feet in Bredth and twenty six feet posts." "Voted to sell the pews in the meeting house before the meeting house is built." (In passing let us read a "transfer" as recorded at this time): "Methuen, December 20, 1796. This certifies that Mr. Jonathan How is the proprietor of one—half the pew No. 44 in the Meeting house built the present year in the first parish in said Methuen & that he the said How hath paid the Sum of Twenty six dollars 75 cts with 16 cts more interest in full for said pew. John Huse & Caleb Swan, Committee."

A building committee of three was chosen. "Voted that four sides and both ends be underpined with hewn stone." The timber was to be cut from the parsonage lot and let out to the lowest bidder. On Jan. 25, 1796, the "meeting was held at Doc. Hildredths Chamber." There was to be no opportunity for "graft." We read the following with interest: The building committee "shall conform themselves to all further instructions from the parish their books and accounts shall always be opened for the perusal of any member of the parish who shall Desire the same and they shall likewise exhibit their accounts to the parish if Desired once in two months until the house is finished and shall be allowed a Reasonable Recompense for their trouble and in case any Disagreement should arise between them and the parish as to their pay the same shall be Referred to three Disinterested men mutually chosen for the purpose which shall be final the payments for the pews were to come at times agreed upon and the vendue was to be held at Doc. Hildreths Chamber". Capt. Caleb Swan was chosen "vendue master." At a meeting in Feb. a few remaining pews in the gallery "were set at twenty dollars each." Also a later vote was that the wood left on the parsonage lot after the removal of the timber be sold to the highest bidder and the money "be laid out for paints and oil to paint the parish Building". On Feb. 11 it was "voted to Build a steeple to the meeting house yeas thirteen nays eleven". At this same meeting a committee was appointed to "apply to the second parish for liberty for our minister to preach in their meeting house while ours is building". Also voted "to build the steeple the east end of the new meeting house."Two shillings were voted James Carleton for "shaving up the meeting house." On April 5, 1796, "voted to take down the old meeting house Twentieth Inst. under the direction of the committee. without any cost to the Parish (rum excepted)." "that the Parish should Glass in ten classes To build a wall through the Parsonage, on the new road." April 23, 1796 "voted to set the new meeting house beck, the north west end, within seven feet of the wall by the road. The nor—east end with the line of the old one." "Voted not to have weight on the windows." (The records tell us that this last meeting was held in "the school house near where the old meeting house stood.") May 11, 1796, "Voted that the workmen should have a breakfast, a dinner & a supper on the parish cost on raising day." "that the carpenters should pick the men and the committee should give them an invitation to raise the sd meeting house." "that the committee should give the spectators a drink or grog on that day." Again quoting from the diary of Rev. William Bentley we read: "by an advertisement on the door of the Meeting House, it is to be taken down on Wednesday April 21, which is the next day. The pews had been taken out, and preparation made. This is their first Meeting House. It was small, and in the usual proportions of our Meeting Houses. Never painted within or without, the timber was on the spot for a new Meeting House, which they expect to raise in May. It is to be upon the plan or the New Meeting House lately finished in the lower Parish of Bradford. With a tower and cupola. The situation is truly delightful. The hill on whose top it is to be placed, rises gently, & the best farms are near it."

The church record reads: "The new meeting-house was raised May 19, 1796 & dedicated to the use of public worship Nov. 3d-1796 & finished by the middle on Nov. 1796. "

On Aug. 13 it was voted to meet in the new meeting house for the first service on the second Sabbath in October. At this same meeting it was voted to audit the accounts of the building committee; also to paint the "parsonage house." The meeting called for Oct. 4 was to be in the school house. This was to reconsider a previous vote regarding the opening of the new "Meeting House." It was decided to postpone such for "the first sabbath in November next". In December a report was rendered by the various committees on building. The books showed "a charge against the Parish of four thousand four hundred and sixty dollars and forty-three cents for labour and articles to build the sd house". "We also find in their book, credit to the sd parish for pews already sold three thousand and fifty seven dollars and also one hundred & sixty two dollars and fifty cents for other articles sold by the committee and also fourteen dollars and seventy five cents paid by David How to Samuel Thom & Ralph Hall 14.75 and there now remains of cost yet to pay One thousand two hundred and forty two dollars and sixteen cents if all the accounts should be allowed in sd book. On Jan. 6, 1797, it was voted "to raise twelve hundred dollars to pay the remaining cost of the meeting house" and "that the parish treasurer give his note on interest from the first day of December last for the materials for the meeting house and for the workmen that did the work. These notes were taken by individuals throughout the parish; even by parties out of town. (Names are recorded of citizens in Haverhill and Andover). One outstanding problem coming up at this time was the repeated request for abatements of the parish tax. We infer from the records of both parishes that such was due to the continued struggle of the second church for its very existence. Couple this with the effort to exact a tax from the same person for the support of both churches and we can easily realize the difficulty in collecting the double tax. In May 1797 there came an innovation worthy mention. "It was voted to have the bass-viol be brought into the meeting house four Sabbaths." As we have noted above, in 1782 the question of "that part of the service called singing" was settled by reading the psalm and the appointment of a choir-master. Later a space was allotted for the choir. But now instrumental music becomes a part of the church service. Just why this kind of a musical instrument should be chosen, we know not; but we do believe that the shades of their ancestors must have been disturbed by such a radical move. In 1804 another striking vote was passed "to find strings for the bass-viol so long as it is kept in the meetinghouse." (A suspicion comes to us that possibly it had been borrowed for outside worldly purposes). Mr. Perley continues to receive his eighty pounds salary. The parsonage "house" needs repairs so it is voted "to repare the harths and whitewash the lower rooms of the parsonage building." And a month later "to whitewash the chambers of the parsonage house." In 1804, there was a vote passed to purchase a certain lot of land near the meeting house of the heirs of Christopher Sargent. With Yankee shrewdness the purchase was brought about by an offer of the parish to buy" grave stones for the Rev. Christopher Sargent and wife provided the heirs give a deed to the first church for the sd land". It would appear from the parish records that the agreement was not reached until 1809 when at a meeting of March 8 we read, "voted to get grave stones for the Rev. Mr. Sargent & his Lady;" also "a committee to purchase the gravestones" consisting of Wm. Swan, Nathaniel Whittier & John Gage. In the Treasurer's Book wider the date Nov. 12, 1810, we read "an order given on the Treasurer to Nathaniel Whittier Eighteen dollars for grave stones for the Rev. Rev. Mr. Sargent and wife also four Dollars for fetching the Sd Stones to the yard." Also on March 5, 1811, "one dollar for Mr. Abial How Cutting Letters on the Revd Mr. Sargent's Grave Stones."

We have spoken frequently of the attempt to divide the town in such a manner that the people have the privilege of attending either church then existing. While the records regarding the smaller parish are fragmentary we do find this as it may concern the First Parish; Feb. 7, 1805, "voted the proposals made by the committee from the first parish in Methuen to the committee from the second parish in sd town giving liberty to all those persons with heir heins and estates that shall establish themselves as above mentioned shall have liberty of Joining either of the parishes in sd town by giving in their names to the town clerk fourteen days at least before next annual town meeting after they purchase in sd town. Also their proportion on non resident land (may be) all that lies on the west side of Spicket river." We infer from this that the much mooted question of a church rate for the inhabitants of the west part is settled. In spite of this, however, a year later a reconsideration was voted and the matter indefinitely settled. From the old book we should judge that John Searl of the northern section west of the Spicket was the leader in the "pole of the parish." Abatement after abatement of taxes due the first parish from those living at a distance had undoubtedly led to these agreements which would appear to have been allowed by the General Court. The general tone of the records is that though the question was not generally settled each institution became separate until the day when the small church and parish could not function and returned to the fold. Let us state that this return was not confined to the First Church. Some went to other churches which by that time existed in town.

The records are well preserved. Hence the space we have given all this.

It is perhaps fitting at this time to speak of some conditions destined to antagonize the Calvinist at the time of the century.

The stern tenets of these beliefs mentioned in Chapter 9 may sound harsh; may fall heavily on our ears. But Calvinism was being beset behind and before. A review of the early faith of our fathers was needed. For more than a century and a half there had existed an antagonism creeping into the church dubbed "The Half-way Covenant." The early Puritan fathers held to the view that only regenerated persons were entitled to full communion and all the privileges of the church. Through household baptism they held that their children were included in the covenant of their parents and in a qualified sense were members of the church. When these children reached maturity and had families of their own, many did not see it to come into the full communion and fellowship of the church and so could not have the ordinance of baptism administered to their children.

How such children could be distinguished from the "Pagans" who might happen to hear the word of God in their assemblies was an issue that was more than disturbing to the grandparents of these infants.

Synods were held at Boston in 1657 and again in 1662. Cotton Mather in his "Magnalia" thus gives us the decision: "Church members who were admitted in minority" (i. e. who were baptized in childhood) "understanding the doctrine of faith and publicly professing their assent thereto not scandalous in life, and solemnly owning the covenant before the church, wherein they give up themselves and their children to the Lord, and subject themselves to the government of Christ, their children are to be baptized". In derision these parents who had been baptized in infancy (children of full communicants) now becoming adults and parents and not obliged to "own the covenant" were dubbed "Half-Way Communicants"——their children likewise.

The ruling adopted by the Haverhill church, (and we judge prevailed in Methuen as well) reads as follows: "Whereas it has been customary for persons in order to obtain baptism for their children, to make a public profession of faith called "owning the Covenant." and as this condition may hinder some persons (though otherwise qualified) from complying with the institution voted, that it be no longer required, but the children of all baptized persons may be admitted to this holy ordinance unless they (the parents) have forfeited this privilege by scandalous immorality."

While it would not be exactly the truth to say, that Congregationalism was experiencing a change, yet other religious sects, even old school. The liberalism of the Socinian was a thorn in the flesh those strictly orthodox but under a new name, were irritants to the to them. Unitarianism had reached out from Boston and Cambridge. The new pastor Perley was suspected of entertaining some of their tenets. In the late nineties of this century the work of Home Missions became an integral part of

Congregational work. In 1808 came the founding of Andover Theological Seminary; built upon the very bed-rock of Calvinism. It was a tower of strength locally. History will bear us out in stating that this was the indirect outcome of the new Unitarian Congregationalism. But the old church remained strictly Trinitarian. This fact undoubtedly kept the Second Parish in existence; nevertheless, this latter body ever had its troubles. In 1810, the American Board of Commissioners for Foreign Missions was organized. This received a sturdy support of the new Andover Seminary; as well drew many able ministers from the local fields.

At the close of Mr. Perley's pastorate the second parish came back into the fold for a short time, but more of this later.

—ELEVEN—

The resignation of Mr. Perley. Some of his experiences.

We would not by any means tire the reader with details connected with these opening years of the nineteenth century, and yet there are certain occurrences in the life of a church and pastor, which in themselves become object lessons to later generations. Any man in a public position is a target for the crowd. Mr. Perley whose pastorate of twenty years was replete with good results, had his failings; his troubles. A minister is human. Sometimes, the layman is not.

Before the writer is a letter, which reads thus:

To the First Parish in Methuen. Sirs

We the subscribers are dissatisfied with Mr. Perley as a in this place and by many things that is stated against him that in our opinion we do believe them to be facts, which is to much for any man to be guilty of, and much more so, for a Gospel Teacher, which is set over us as a Watchman Upon the Walls of Jerusalem, for one that must give an account how he has taught his People, and to have thing Remain so, we are unwilling to do and to have Mr. Perley Continue, and thing remain unsettled we regret to Say, that a Sepperatron must take place, on our own part, for we do think it must be a great wound to the cause of Christ in Supporting; man of his Character in the Works of a Minister

This letter is signed by eight well known men of the parish. On March 17, 1810, a special meeting of the parish had been called at the request "of a committee to see if the parish will vote to concur with said church in calling a council of inquiry and advice to inquire into the evil stores circulated about the Revd. Mr. Perley and act thereon as the parish shall think proper." The article was thrown down, On July 23 of the same year there appeared an approaching crisis regar mg the issue with Mr. Perley. At meeting it was voted to concur with the church and. "call a council on account of the difficulties with the Rev. Mr. Perley." A committee of three Joseph How, Abiel How and John Gage to "agree with the church." The report of the Parish Treasurer, Peter Marston on March 27, had shown a year's salary "beginning Oct. 18, 1808" "due to Mr. Perley" "excepting twenty four dollars and sixty-two cents which he has received?" In March, 1811 this was still unpaid.

At this council seven ministers each to bring a delegate were present from as many towns roundabout: Mr. Peabody of Atkinson, Allen out Bradford, Church of Pelham, Tompkins of Haverhill, Eaton of Boxford, Smith of Salem, N. H. and Dodge of Haverhill. That this council was a somewhat long drawn out affair is evinced by this order drawn on the treasurer: "to Daniel Fry Thirty Six Dollars, it being for Bording Council three days in October 1810." We cannot take the space to enter into detail concerning the existing difficulties between pastor and people. His salary was voted each year but for the last three years, it appears on the records as unpaid.

On Oct. 10, 1810, the council met in due form with Rev. Stephen Peabody as moderator and Rev. Jonathan Allen and Rev. John Smith scribes. The charges brought forward by the few members of the church and parish were: (1) Perley is charged with taking sundry boards from the fence or enclosure of Isaac Bodwell without his knowledge or consent "in particular some boards near the barn where Henry Bodwell, Jr. now lives". (2)

"Perley is charged w1th prevarications respecting said boards, with an intention to deceive mid church and parish". (3) Said Perley is charged "with taking and using horses of his neighbors found in his vicinity without knowledge or consent of the owners." (A foot note in the records explains this act as follows: "Mr. Elijah Carlton's horse where said Perley had before lived a year went in the high way & happened one morning to come to his door; under a kind of a necessity he took the horse and carried two of his little children to school half a mile & turned the horse out. The second horse broke into sd Perley's. Pasture & he by a previous agreement with the man that owned the horse used him a little; sent word to the man & paid him previously for the horse. The third horse broke into sd Perley's pasture & laid there, some days he took the horse up & rode him two miles to find an owner principally & to accompany sick child to the doctor. This was known before the complainers joined the church three years before the complaint".) (4) "They charge said Perley with falsehood respecting said horses with an intent to deceive the people & exculpate himself." (5) "They charge sd Perley with diverse imprudencies in conversation & conduct among his parishioners in inter-meddling with business not connected with parochial duties."

The council carefully examined all the above charges. Nothing of an incriminating nature was found worthy consideration. Under the number 5 they admit that Mr. Perley might have been more discreet in his conversation. They cite as an example the instance when in a conversation with Nathaniel Whittier a previous collector for the parish he was accused by said Whittier of being behind in his parish calls, Perley replied by asking Whittier if he "was any more behind in his calls than he (Whittier) was in paying the minister. This salary." For two years Whittier had been collector with money available, yet had not paid Perley his salary during that time. He had not turned the money over to the treasurer so that Perley was "reduced to straits." "Could he (Perley) make bricks without straw?"

Mr. Perley was declared innocent of the charges brought by men indifferent, so they thought, regarding the welfare of the church. He was a man human as are all men. The church should go on with a worthy interest in the greater things of life and leave behind the trivial matters of the day. Even though the pastor endeavored to bring about a reconciliation, such was not accomplished. Later Whittier moved to south Andover. "When Daniel Fry and wife and Bailey Davis and wife found they could not be dismissed from the first church of Christ to the second church in Methuen they immediately took to the ana-baptists and preachers, worried along with them holding night meetings and conferences proclaiming their goodness and complaining of the congregational order & regular ministers until the 13th of June 1814 when they were baptized by immersion by one Williams of Beverley in Spicket river near Thomas Hericks. What these people will be or turn to next the Lord only knows. This is written for the church hereafter. A double minded man is unstable in all his ways." (We read that before they united with the anabaptists an unsuccessful effort was made to Join the Haverhill association for honorable dismission). A side record tells us that on "the 8th of March 1815 the above named Daniel Fry & wife & Bailey Davis & wife with number of others were incorporated into a Baptist church, set up in Methuen by Dr. Baldwin of Boston, Mr. Batchelder of Haverhill & an ex minister of the order from Beverley, Mass. this was just five years to one day after these people formerly made their first difficulty with their pastor by investigating a church meeting."

But the strain had been severe for Mr. Perley; for a man to serve his people for twenty years and then be brought before the bar of ecclesiastical justice for trivial human misdemeanor is an experience somewhat bordering on the criminal. Our New England church had its sources of strength. At the same time the theocratic rule, exceeding that of the magistrate temporal, had gotten such a grip on the Puritanic mind that the proverbial angel dancing on a needle's point was too often an object of scrutiny. But one result could be expected. The church was to give way in order to retain its strength or to weaken through a stubborn resistance. Temporarily it appeared to take the latter course.

To say that Perley was entirely blameless would not be true. At times he was too free with his words. To illustrate: While the Baptist Society was building, a committee from that church sought the use of the "meeting house of the first church" for the old matron of their first minister, Mr. Charles O. Kimball. A decided denial was returned. The idea persisted in the mind of Mr. Perley for at the time of reading his resignation, he felt called upon to strike a final blow as follows: "If they have now done with me, they have the Almighty to deal with; who will meet out to them according as they have measured to others; the waters of the Spicket will not wash away their sins." "Will they not strive to take your house of God in possession & to convert your public property to their own use? From the first settlement of this church and parish they have EVER HAD their IMPLACABLE Those who have rung up among, speaking perverse things to draw away disciples after them. But never had you more subtle adversaries than at the present day. Societies of different denominations are formed round about and no pains are spared, whether right or wrong, to gain Proselytes; and their success depends on our destruction. tis or their existence to destroy yours, as a society; of this their conduct shows them not insensible. Poor, illiterate, ignorant men have invaded the priest's office, like Uzziah of old, pretending to offer holy incense in the Sanctuary of God. Some are idling about from house to house and, creeping in, they lead away silly women laden with their sins." "In proportion to the increase of various sectarics and vagabond preachers, have been the judgments and calamities and miseries of our country." (From Rev. King Solomon Hall's *History of the Baptist Church*").

The records tell us that Mr. Perley "requested a dismission which was granted May 24, 1815." The church voted "to pay up all back arrearages and give Mr. Perley 250 dollars in one year. There were no charges brought against him notwithstanding all that had been pretended and he obtained of the Counsel honorable recommendation." Let us read it from the records:

> The First Church of Christ in Methuen resolve, that the groundless disaffection, (to give it no harsher term,) of some of its late members, now gone out from us, and a part of the parishioners, was the cause of the separation of this church and their Rev. Pastor. Therefore, they view with regret, their separation. But as the circumstances of support have made it necessary for them to apart with their beloved Pastor, the Rev. Humphrey C. Perley, whom they view as a worthy minister of the New Testament, and since things, in Divine Providence, have taken place, they desire humbly to submit to the will of God, and most cordially recommend him to the Churches of Christ, where God in his righteous Providence, may call him to minister in holy things.

> A true copy Richard Messer, Chh. clerk

From the Church Manual we read that Mr. Perley served the church in Beverley, Mass. from 1818 to 1821. He died in 1838 at the age of seventy-six.

The First Church of Christ, as the old parish and church organization is now called, is again without a leader.

—TWELVE—

THE FOURTH MINISTER REV. JACOB WEED EASTMAN. A NEW CREED. UNION WITH THE SECOND PARISH. EVANGELISM AND MISSIONS, ORDINATION OF ABIJAH CROSS, JR.

But the church was more active in choosing a successor than had been the case in the past. About four months after the dismissal of Mr. Perley we read that the parish was asked to concur in the choice of Mr. Jacob Weed Eastman as pastor. This was on Sept. 12, 1815. Harmony prevailed. On Nov. 14 following, arrangements were made for calling an ecclesiastical council for Dec. 13 at the home of Lieut. John Gage. The examination proving satisfactory, the council proceeded to the meeting house. We note representatives from all the neighboring churches excepting Andover. Just why that town was omitted, we cannot explain.

Mr. Eastman was born in Sandwich, N. H. We read that he was not a college graduate. Different accounts mention him as a rugged man physically, from the New Hampshire hills; clean morally and exceedingly strict in his religious views. During his pastorate extending over thirteen and a half years, the spiritual welfare of the church and parish was surely first and last in his mind. An early vote was that there should be seven communion services in one year. At this same meeting, the first in the new pastorate, the male members present contributed the sum of one dollar and forty cents "to purchase a new church book, and have the covenant of the Church written in it, and have all the present members sign their names in it, and all who shall hereafter be admitted, shall sign the stone." On Feb. 25, 1816 an agreement was brought about between the first and second parishes that they unite as one ("except in cases of discipline") for one year. Deacon William Bodwell of the second church with John Pettingill as substitute, were chosen to "sit" with the deacons of the first church "in the deacons' seats." On Dec. 13, 1816 the "New Creed" was drawn up to conform with the Cambridge Platform. The New England theocracy was still holding its own, although individualism was slowly creeping in. As before stated the "Half-way Covenant" was a constant irritant to Calvinism.

May we at this time mention a custom characteristic of the close adherence to church discipline and order. We cite directly from the records: "As a mark of respect to our beloved brother Dea. William Swan voted that we will pay our last respects by following him to the grave as mourners." Also "voted that brother Richard Messer be requested to invite the Musical Society in this place to attend the funeral of our deceased brother". "Voted that brother Job Pingree be requested to invite Mr. Phineas Messer to superintend the music on said day." On Jan. 23, 1817 the second church was accepted into full communion with the old Parish and "On April 16 the two parishes united as one tender the name of THE UNITED CHURCH." Richard Messer was chosen clerk. There were to be three "Ruling Elders", viz: William Bodwell, William Runnels and John Pettengill. Two deacons were chosen: Timothy Emerson of the first and Robert Hastings of the second parish church. At this time a "preparatory lecture"- was held each season prior to the communion. Voted it be "incumbent on every communicant to attend lectures preparatory to communion and that without urgent reason, none have a right to absent themselves." On Jan. 4, 1818, there is an interesting record indicative of the desire to hold the regular service of the church regardless any ordinary contingency. "If any Sabbath should find the pulpit destitute of a minister then the elders or deacons should assume the authority to choose some suitable person to lead in prayer, read Tor singing and read to the congregation assembled any person acceptable to the people."

As an example of the sincerity, piety and close adherence to the early Covenant, let us instance a "church meeting holden at the meeting house July 3, 1820." "Attended to the application of Jonas Richardson requesting that the church creed and confession of faith may be so modified that he may be received to communion while destitute of a hope of having experienced a change of heart, and voted that Elder Bodwell, Deacon Smitt and Elder Runnels be a committee to labor with said Richardson and urge him to embrace the Gospel." "After attending to the relations of Moses Merrill and Hannah his wife, voted they be pronounced for communion. "The subject of a fast to pray for the outpouring of the Spirit was proposed and referred to a church meeting to be holden on Friday next week. The Church then resolved itself into a concert of prayer." Some two years later "Brother" Richardson above mentioned was received into full communion. We read that in cases similar to this, weekly meetings were held at the call of the pastor; quite generally held at the "parsonage house."

In 1820, it was voted "that in addition to the communion heretofore established the church will commune on the third Sabbath in Feb and Dec. The spirit of evangelism and the cause of missions were fostered in those early days of the church as thus evinced: monthly meetings were arranged "for promoting a revival of religion" and "when any messengers delegated to attend to represent this church he unable to attend, that they appoint substitutes to go in their places." Again in 1822, a special contribution was taken for the education of a heathen child in Ceylon." During this year nine Communion services were held. Jan. 1 of 1823 was voted "a day of fasting and prayer to implore the outpouring of the Spirit on this place the ensuing year."

Of local interest is the fact that several young men have gone out from our church to enter the ministry. The first recorded is in connection with a letter-missive received from Salisbury, N.H. requesting the assistance of this church by pastor and delegate "in ordaining Abijah Cross, Jr. over them," Mr. Cross had been previously incensed by the Haverhill Association. He remained at Salisbury five years. After which he came to West Haverhill church as stated supply for two years. Installed there May 18, 1831 he remained until his dismissal Jan. 26, 1853. A letter to the Council at the time of his installation in the Haverhill church tells us that he was born in Methuen, Oct. 25, 1793. Inasmuch as this was the first member of our church to enter the ministry, (we shall mention others later), it may be fitting to give the leading statements of this letter: "My parents were Abijah Cross of Methuen, and Eliza Parker of Dracut." "My grandparents on my father's side were William Cross of Methuen and Mary Corliss of Salem, N.H. My maternal grandparents lived and died in Dracut." "In the line of my father I am a German of the fifth generation." "In his early life he "had studied medicine with Ralph Harris of Methuen." Changing views on religion led him to study Latin and Greek with Daniel Noyes; later with Mr. Greenlief both of Bradford; studied at Middlebury and Dartmouth Colleges: taught school for some years, (to pay his debts of of out $250.00), at Sanborn Academy in Ashfield, Mass. Continuing his religious work to some extent in the school, he entered Andover Theo. Seminary in 1822 for four months; later studying with Rev. E. L. Parker of Derry and Rev. Daniel Dana, D. D. of Londonderry.

On June 1, 1827, a letter-missive was received from the newly formed church in West Andover. "Elder Swan," with Elder Bodwell substitute, was chosen delegate with the pastor to represent the church. at the ordination of Mr. Samuel Cram Jackson on June 26, 1827. The pastor of the Methuen church "offered prayer" at this service. (Mr. Jackson was the first minister of the newly organized West Parish Church in Andover.

On Aug. 22, 1827, a baptismal bowl was presented the church by Miss Sarah V. Hosmer.

On July 4, 1828, Mr. Eastman read his resignation to the church assembled. It was accepted and Mr. Eastman given a true and sincere recommendation as a "faithful and Successful minister of the New Testament and endorsed as such to all churches." Thus closes a pastorate of twelve successful years. From the records we judge pence and harmony existed. An earnest zeal for spiritual work appears to have continued under his leadership. He went from this church to North Reading, Mass. thence to Rocky Springs, Ohio.

—THIRTEEN—

THE SUNDAY SCHOOL. REV. SPENCER FIELD BEARD. DEVELOPMENT AT SPICKETT FALLS. MEETING-HOUSE MOVED FROM THE "COMMON". SECOND PARISH REORGANIZED. REV. SYLVESTER G. PIERCE.

With an experience somewhat different from the past, the church immediately selects a successor. As just stated, the people were working in harmony. The inception of a Sunday School appears during the ministry of Mr. Eastman. We believe that such has been and is today the direct means of maintaining the vitality of the church. The youth is brought into closer touch with the working of their best interests. The influence of the Andover Seminary must have been felt in our town. We read that many of its students had been "supplying" the pulpit; consequent a comparatively easy matter to bring candidates before the people. Furthermore other church (the Baptist and Universalist) were well established in town so that it was best to be as expeditious as possible in keeping the work uninterrupted. At any rate, in about two months (or to be exact, on Sept. 1.) the church voted an "invitation" to Mr. Spencer Field Beard "to settle in the work of Christ" in the "First Church of Christ" in Methuen — as well to ask the parish to concur in this action; which was promptly done; with a vote to allow Mr. Beard a salary of $500.00. On Jan. 5, 1829, a letter-missive was sent to the neighboring churches and on Jan. 21 the exercises of ordination took place.

Spencer Field Beard, son of Dr. David and Betsey (Field) Beard was born in West Brookfield, Mass. July 4, 1799. Graduated from Amherst College in 1824 and Andover Theological Seminary in 1827. He was Agent of the American Board for one year 1827-8. Mr. Beard's pastorate was short; but a few months over three years. An exceedingly spiritual man, his work was strictly in accord with the tenets of the old church. During 1829, we find recorded but one accession. In 1830, four admitted by letter and one restored to full communion. During 1831, twenty-one were received on concession of faith.

On March 7, 1832, at a meeting of the church held at the home of Benjamin Osgood Mr. Beard's resignation was read and accepted. We are not told the particulars of so short a pastorate. That he stood well with his people is evinced in the vote that he "be recommended to the Council to be called as an affectionate and faithful minister of the New Testament and that they be requested to recommend him as such to the churches. On April 25, 1832, the Council met; dissolved the relations between church and pastor and strongly urged the church to be as expeditious as possible in securing a successor. After leaving this parish, Mr. Beard held several pastorates in Connecticut and was for five years at Waquoit, Mass. In 1853, he moved to Andover, on the "Hill;" there to reside until his death in 1876.

He is buried in the Chapel Cemetery on Andover Hill. A grandson of Mr. Beard, William Spencer Beard, was a classmate of the writer at Andover Academy. He is now Chairman of the LAYMAN'S ADVISORY COMMITTEE connected with the National Council of the Congregational Churches of America. We shall hope to have him with us at the Anniversary.

During the year in which Mr. Beard closes his pastorate and Mr. Pierce succeeds, the development of the town had reached a Faint when it became evident that the real center was to be at the falls. On the banks of the Spicket had sprung up the inception of the textile industry destined to mark this region as the coming manufacturing section of eastern New England. The Methuen Company, Inc. as early as 1820 had developed the power of the Spicket. In 1825, 8000 yards of ticking were each month put on the market. The manufacture of hats and shoes was also a living industry so that here in our present Methuen center, men saw the very heart of the town. All this of course meant that the old church must conform to the changing conditions. Wilson's Hall (on the south corner of High and Hampshire Streets) was used by the Universalist Society. The Baptists were well established in their first church building on the spot now occupied by that society.

We are ready to believe that much opposition from the eastern section existed. For more than a hundred years, each Sabbath saw men wending their way up to the "Hill" to their "meeting house." On this Common (a term sometimes used) lay their ancestors in God's Acre. To move down to the Falls, we imagine was unthinkable. However, in 1832 the plan to move was definitely agreed upon, but the same building was to be used.

This structure erected in 1796 was carefully taken down and moved to the lot now occupied by this beautiful house of granite. On another page, we present a cut of this re-established structure and chapel adjoining. The details concerning the removal are not in our possession; due to the missing records of the parish covering those years. An interesting item found in the records of the town reads: "March 4, 1833 voted that the Town relinquish their right and title of the Land where the Meeting House of the First Parish in Methuen has been removed from to the Episcopal Society for the purpose of erecting a Meeting House if any right they have." We find no further record regarding the matter and so judge they did not have the "right" and so dropped the case allowing the land to revert to the town by which it was originally granted.

April 8 of the previous year a letter was received from "The Second Parish" in Methuen asking that the First Church assist in ordaining Mr. Josiah Hill to the work of the ministry in the west part of the town." The fact that this second parish was endeavoring to re-establish itself was undoubtedly a spur to the old parish to assert its influence unbroken. The advice of the council mentioned above had evidently been anticipated for on April 16 scarcely more than a week before the meeting of that council, the church voted "unanimously to give the Rev. Sylvester G. Pierce a call to become their pastor." A salary of $700.00 was voted the new minister.

Mr. Pierce was a clergyman of several years of religious experience. Born in Wilmington, Vt. in 1797, he had early in life been a keen and earnest worker in evangelism. The Presbyterian Church with its rigid Calvinism appealed to him. Attending Union College in Schenectady, he proved a pupil of superior rank. At the commencement of his senior year, he felt the call for work in the foreign fields. Conferring with the American Board for Foreign Missions, he entered Andover Seminary. Having previously served the church in Cohasset, he found his work in the Seminary conducive to carrying on evangeliatic teaching in surrounding towns. In 1828 he commenced what proved to be a four year's pastorate in West

Dracut. Contrary to his previous intentions, he was there ordained. His proximity to Methuen brought about an acquaintance which reinstalled in his being installed pastor in this church June 27, 1832. Sometime previously, his health had been very poor. However, after a rest, he had again taken up his work. During a pastorate of seven years, his leadership here was wonderfully blessed. In 1837, he was more or less absent from his pulpit owing to the re-occurrence of a lung trouble. Going to a sanatorium, he returned in the spring of 1833. On the first Sunday of 1839, he preached what proved to be his last sermon. He died May 8, 1839 at the age of forty-two. He is buried in Walnut Grove Cemetery.

Mr. Pierce's pastorate proved especially fruitful. During the year 1832, twenty nine persons were received into the church by profession of faith and nine by letter. At this time, the communion service was held on alternate months commencing with the first Sunday in January. During 1833, twenty-four come into the church by profession and four by letter. It must be repeated here that the reception of a member was only after a strict examination of a thorough change of heart from the world and a deep knowledge of the doctrines of the Christian faith. Events procedure was demanded of those received by letter from other churches. During this pastorate several members were dropped from the roll for dances discovered in their daily lives. During this ministry one hundred fifty were added to the church of whom one hundred thirteen were by profession. Space alone prevents us from citing the beautiful testimonial incorporated into the records relative to the work of Mr. Pierce. This was a time when the so-called "hard times" existed throughout the country; but with a prayer "that men may feel that wealth is but a matter of the present" the church as a whole felt the Christian duty to take hold and lift "so that men may see the beauty of the eternal."

—FOURTEEN—

On November 26, 1839, a letter was sent Rev. John C. Phillips at the time pastor in Weymouth, Mass. This communication fairly begs Mr. Phillips, to seriously consider the desire of the Methuen people to seek his services. The church had (through the illness of Mr. Pierce) "been deprived of ministerial labor." Many cases of discipline had been brought before the church. A strong leader was needed and men in general felt that Mr. Phillips was the one leader for the parish. The letter closes with these words: "We believe the people desire an affectionate Pastor's counsel, sympathy, and prayers; and that an early and favorable answer would be received in a spirit of thanksgiving to the great Head of the Church." The reply of Mr. Phillips was one of acceptance promising the people his best with the deep desire to promote the interests of church and parish.

A salary of $800.00 was granted Mr. Phillips. We are told that he built the house neat east of the present residence of Mr. John D. Emerson, and there lived during a portion of his pastorate continuing more than twenty years. This salary was to be paid in quarterly installments. In addition, he was allowed "four Sabbaths for vacation.

We are now entering upon an era when the social and religious life in our town is well established. By 1840, the industrial interests have a recognition throughout the world. The Methuen Lyceum was a factor in the educational life. There was a circulating library; a local newspaper had been published for several years. In 1839, a private high school held its sessions in the vestry of our church. In 1841, there was such a school in which the town met one half the cost. In 1838, we read the announcement of a concert given by the local brass band in the Congregational Church. While mentioning the question of music, we wonder how many of our readers know anything about the "ophicleide". On May 4, 1841, we is read that "Albert Smith had an order on the treasurer for twenty-five dollars for an ophicleide for the use of said parish." Let us state that it was a kind of trumpet; doubtless, used in leading the singing in church services; as is the cornet this day.

The progress of the town called for leaders in its churches. In Mr. Phillips, we find that the old church contributed such leadership. This, the seventh pastor, of our church was born in Boston; his father John Phillips was the first mayor of that city; his brother Wendell, the well known orator and anti-slavery leader. John, who was to be the pastor in Methuen for over twenty years had spent several years in the study of law; but changing his plans he entered Andover Seminary where he was graduated in 1832. His first pastorate was at Weymouth where he was ordained the year following graduation. Here he remained until taking up work in this town. He was installed here Dec. 25, 1839.

At this distance, it would appear to the reader that a clergyman from Unitarian Beacon Street might, to a certain extent, be at variance with the Calvinism of the old Methuen church. We are however of the opinion that with the experience of the years when the second parish broke away from the first also with the new denominations now existing in a rapidly growing center, that denominational difference became not so outstanding; that a strong man could steer the ship away from the attempts to "split the hair."

We cannot detail the work of Mr. Phillips and the church as a. whole during the generations to follow. The records clearly tell us that it was a strong pastorate. A few outstanding activities may be touched upon. Early in this period, it was voted to hold the annual meeting of the church "in the month of May;" at which the clerk, treasurer, and standing committee were to be chosen. Members or the church in good standing "who shall leave the church and town for any length of time" "must take letters of membership with them." Collections shall be taken at each communion service "for the benefit of the church." Cases of discipline repeatedly came up at the church meetings. Many were "excommunicated." Several members were occasionally dismissed to other churches in town. A decided stand for the temperance movement was taken with suggestions that each member, "sign the total abstinence pledge." A firm attitude was taken in support of the "anti-slavery movement." Charity was continually practiced throughout the parish. The church was ever ready to contribute to the support of its needy "providing the case were not too prolonged;" in which case they were placed in the "town farm." In 1838, the Town had purchased the Nathaniel Sargent farm for its paupers. This was situated in the present Lawrence section; between Bradford and Haverhill streets (now so called) extending west toward the Tower Hill district.

The Sunday School becomes a strong asset of the church. While this department had been a factor since the days of Mr. Eastman, the institution was more or less informal with no definite organization. In 1836, during Mr. Pierce's pastorate there were about one hundred pupils in nine classes. We are in possession of the records of that period. Careful attention was paid to attendance; as well were regular reports given by teachers and superintendent or the progress steadily made. A well-equipped library was maintained; at one time counting one thousand volumes. A well-regulated work in missions was carried on in both the Home and Foreign fields. At this time during the ministry of Mr Phillips, in 1811, we read that there were three hundred four pupils enrolled in thirty-one classes. The important fact connected with the Sunday School during those years, as well as later, was the existence of classes for adults. The value of the church-school is that it knows no graduation. The old as well as the youth should be an integral part of this phase of the church life. Much valuable work has been done along these lines. For many years, the so-called "Josephine Emerson Class" was a wonderful asset to our church life. The records show us a membership of over forty ladies, who for many years sustained this work in the School. Mrs. Emerson was the wife of Jacob Emerson, Jr. a deacon of the church for more than thirty years and outstanding leader in the parish. Surely we must admit that these were days when the church functioned in all departments; when this old organization of a century and a quarters growth was a real factor in the town and when the labor of those "gude men and true" was being strongly supported. Any church should feel proud of the following report which we take from the church-records: at the annual meeting in 1843 "the average attendance of the Sunday School for the past year was one hundred ninety one, with one hundred eighty nine reported for the previous year". The report of church benevolences was equally good: $200.00 "were collected for the American Board." Twenty dollars "for the child in Ceylon." For the Seamen's Friend Society $16.89. For Home Missions $125.75. American Tract Society $22.63. Communion collections $27.84. From several monthly concerts $35.37. There were thirteen different fields of work for benevolences; among these we read of Armenians, Jews, slaves, Indians "and others." All these were grouped under six heads and two monthly collections for each taken during the   Let us state that at this time there were three missionary societies connected with the church; Gentlemen's, Ladies' Associations for Foreign Missions and a Junior Society contributing to the "child in Ceylon." The entire amount collected for the fiscal year ending May 8, 1851 was $434.33. The reader must understand that these were from the church organizations and for benevolence, not from the parish which was and is today a district part of our‧ organization taking care of the parish expenses only. Considering the day and the times, we believe the above figures will favorable compare with those of our churches this day. Considering the apparent strength of the church at that time, we cannot deny that he "who gives, receives." A church that interests itself in kindred matters outside of its own self, cannot but receive its own good.

—FIFTEEN—

CONSTRUCTION OF PRESENT CHURCH BUILDING. REV. E. H. GREELEY.

We have left until the last what was the outstanding event during the pastorate of Mr. Phillips. The "meeting house" of wooden construction moved bodily from its original site on the "Hill" in 1632 was to be replaced by one granite. In 1853, the old structure was torn down. The accompanying print shows us the venerable building that had been the spiritual home for fifty seven years. (Yes, for most of that time the civic center as well). As stated above this had stood on the "Hill" or "common" where, built in 1796, it had replaced the original structure of 1729. As also mentioned before, it was voted "to build a steeple on the east end" patterned alter "the new meeting house lately finished in the tower parish of Bradford." This evidently became a type for the new stone structure. We are told by the older residents of the town that plan for this new tower were drawn or suggested by a certain Frank Lathe. From the little we can gather, this man was a stranger who had settled in the town; a school-teacher holding his classes in the old vestry or chapel. The original plans called for a tower eight feet higher; the change was made while building. With but little need for repairs, this work has stood the blasts of the years; a wonderful monument to the workmanship and architecture of the last century. Many members of the parish point with pride to the tower as they recall the names of ancestors having an active part in its construction. The old wooden church was entirely demolished. The vestry or chapel was moved to one side and within the memory of many now living used as a center for social and religious gatherings. It was eventually moved to the west side of Railroad street; later, back facing Pearl Court where it now stands as a store house.

The church was dedicated on Wednesday October 3, 1855, a program of the exercises is before me as I write. It includes "Dedication Anthem" written by the pastor, Mr. Phillips. There are seven numbers on this program. At the bottom of the sheet we read, "The sale of Pews in this House will take place tomorrow. Thursday, at 1 o'clock P. M."

Of local interest, we find the following figures in an old treasure's book. (We wish the parish records were available: but they are missing).

"Sold the bell" $299.00
"Net proceeds from the old meeting house" 169.00
"Organ sold to Rev. Mr. Page" 160.00
"Lawrence St. Ch. Contrib. lamps (value)" 75.00
"Contrib. for Bibles & Hymn books" 45.63
"Contrib. for carpeting Church" 344.25
"Bills paid on the building 9427.48
"Cost of furnishing estimating values of donations included" 1885.45
"Paid S. P. Simmons (contract work)" 6332.12
"Total cost of the building" 15759.60
"Total cost of furniture" 1885.45
Total cost" 17645.05
"Receipts-contributions etc. sale of bell etc. & donations" 12491.22
"Total debt" 5153.83
The above is an exact copy of the page in the treasurer's book.

Let us state that the sum of $4750.00 was immediately raised by personal notes against the parish by a dozen members. Mr. Phillips himself held a note of $1000.00. In 1858, a "windfall" came to the parish in the form of a bequest of $1300.00 from Stephen Hastings, in memory of his father Robert Hastings, a former member, and faithful worker in many religious interests. This was given with the stipulation that it be used toward "building the new church."

Mr. Phillips was a leading factor in Methuen and the surrounding towns throughout his .pastorate of two decades. He was an ardent worker in the cause for temperance. During the early years of his term of service, the town was disturbed by the promiscuous sale of liquor especially on the New Hampshire border where the laws had not been rigidly enforced. A strong Temperance Society was organized. The town records tell us of a stringent law passed to enforce police action; also of many incendiary fires caused by the bitter feelings amused. The churches in town as a unit joined in the crusade. Mr. Phillips a trained lawyer, and naturally an orator, led the forces. On the "first Thursday evening in January 1854" occurred the formal dedication of the present town house. The chief address was given by Mr. Phillips.

On March 26, 1860, the beloved pastor sent his letter of resignation to the church. The question of his health was the paramount issue. The people were reluctant to accept the decision of their leader and so voted. A committee waited on Mr. Phillips with the plan to arrange in some way for his continuance with them. But their efforts were of no avail. On April 13, the resignation was formally accepted. The council met on May 16. 1860, and dismissed the pastor.

The interregnum was to be of short duration. On December 3, of the same year an attempt on the part of the parish was made to call a Mr. Peck to the pastorate. Disagreements with the church as well as some members of the parish itself led to a break in the negotiations. On January 4, of the following year an agreement was reached by which a call was extended the Rev. E. H. Greeley, of late pastor of the Pearl Street Church in Nashua. His acceptance soon followed. He was duly installed by council March 7, 1861. Mr. Greeley was a native of Hopkinton, N. H. He was graduated from Dartmouth College in 1845; and Andover Theological Seminary in 1849. This was his third pastorate. He remained here a little over five years. Unlike Mr. Phillips, who was obliged to retire from the active ministry at the close of his work here, Mr. Greeley continued his work and later became the Secretary of the New Hampshire Missionary.

—SIXTEEN—

ENLARGEMENT OF VESTRY. THE CHURCH DEBT. COLLECTING THE PEW-TAX.

At the annual meeting in May, 1860, Jacob Emerson, Jr. was elected Treasurer and I. H. Laney re-elected Clerk. In July arrangements were under way for the enlargement of the vestry. Illustrative of the fidelity shown by the old church at a time when the Civil War was drawing upon the very vitality of the home-life, we cite these figures from the books: "From the funds in the bands of the treasurer, $40.00 appropriated toward the cost of the new vestry." At the annual meeting in 1863 the total receipts from all departments of the church (not parish) amounted to $640.76. The old town was in the front ranks, in New Hampshire's response to President Lincoln's call, for help in preserving the union. The continual draft on the town treasury for bounties and state aid-as well as for local emergencies, must have necessarily been felt in meeting the expenses of the church and parish. At the annual parish meeting in April 1861, the debt was recorded as $5864 22. However, we don't read of the people throwing up their hands in despair, (The larger part of the debt consisted of notes held by different members of the parish). We do not read of a movement to cut the minister's salary. On the other hand, where Mr. Phillips had received a salary of $800.00, his successor Mr. Greeley was voted $1000.00 and "a vacation of four Sabbaths." In 1861 (as we have just noted), the "vestry" was enlarged and repaired at a cost of $274.86 is expenditure was met by popular subscription. An interesting phase of this free-will contribution is recorded in the old books. We read, for instance, of a certain amount $700.00 raised by subscription; and the statement: "each member was asked and expected to give what the soliciting committee thought the individual was able to give. Such a scheme might have worked in the sixties. We wonder how it would be today.

We must not forget that one source of revenue of the church (in addition to these subscriptions) was the inevitable "pew-tax." As regards the collection of such, the laws of "the Medea and Persians" prevailed. At the commencement of the parish, practically all the pews were owned by its members. Changing conditions brought about changing laws. The enlargement of the meeting-house, inability of many to meet their obligations, many leaving town, some parties desiring to hire sittings; all these were problems; But the one law unchanged was that if a man owned a pew, he must pay the tax. All the pews were appraised— in the gallery and on the floor. In 1858, a tax of 6% was fixed as the rate. Later it was raised to 10%. This was usually payable one-half on June 1 and the other on December 1. The reader must understand that this was to be paid, too. There was no equivocation or reservation. It did not mean that the collector would call again. Here is a sample of the "call" taken from an old book in 1818:

To Capt Joshua Buswell Treasurer for the first parish in Methuen

—Sir we have assessed the sum of three hundred and seventy-seven dollars twenty seven cents on the polls and estates of the First Parish in Methuen and committed the same to lesse Sargent collector for said parish with a warrant requiring him to levy and collect the same, and to pay the same to you in your said capacity-or-your successor in said office. You are therefore to demand and receive of the said collector the above sum on or before the first day of October next—Which sum you are to pay out as follows (viz) To the Rev. Jacob W. Eastman his salary for the present year two hundred and sixty seven dollars—and the remainder you are to pay as you are hereafter directed—$377.27.

December 17th. 1818
Enoch Poor
Peter Marston
Jona. Currier
Assessors for said Parish

A reasonable length of time would allow for emergencies, but when the parish felt that such had elapsed, then came execution in this wise: (We take it directly from the records.)

"In the name of the Commonwealth of Massachusetts"—— "and if any person shall refuse or neglect to pay the tax he is assessed and set in said list, to distrain the goods and chattels of such persons to the value thereof and the distrain so taken to keeip for the space of four days at the cost and charge of the owner an if he shall not pay the same so assessed within the four days, then you are to sell at public vendue, the distrain so taken for the payment thereof with charges, first giving forth eight hours. Notice thereof by Posting up Notifications thereof in some Publick place in said Parish. And the overplus arising from said sale, if any there be besides the sum of said assessment and cost of taking and keeping such distraint you are to immediately to restore to the owner, and for want of goods or chattels whereof to make distraint (besides tools or implements necessary for his Trade or occupation—beasts of the plow necessary for the cultivation and utensils for house-keeping necessary for upholding life. Bedding and apparel necessary for himself and Family) for the space of twelve days you are to take the body of the Person so refusing or neglecting and him to commit to the common jail of the County, there to remain until he pays the same or such part thereof and shall not be abated by the assessors for the time being"

Such savors of the old world; imprisonment for debt was in vogue right here in our New England; and this scarcely more than a century since.

We can easily imagine that many pews were taken over by the parish; and such was the case. From those days we have slowly evolved the plan of church ownership; finally yielding them up altogether and adopting the "free pew" arrangement. It was but a few years ago that the last owner surrendered his pew to the church.

—SEVENTEEN—

In 1863, the church dept stood at $5666.27. During these years, we find that small amounts were appropriated for the "use of the singing choir." Occasionally, there were years when no appropriations were made. On April 5, 1864, we find a vote "to pay $52.00 for playing the organ;" evidently one dollar each Sunday during the year. In the early seventies, we find the name of Miss Helen Simonds organist. At the time of voting this amount for the organist's salary, we read "nothing for the singing choir." This was not due to any apathy toward the question of vocal music. On the other hand there were signs of a super-abundance of interest. A disturbance existed in the church choir, (not unknown in modern times.) Two members seem to have been the cause of the discontent. Their tenure of office was undesirable—to some. Affairs came to such a pass that a public word of apology" was voted "in order to restore harmony needed. In April 1865, it was voted "to take a collection some time during the year for singing and one for lighting and warming the church." Mr. Henry Webster was chosen for that position by the assessors with the stipulation that he "fill up the choir." An appropriation of $250,00 was made for singing for that year.

It was during the pastorate of Mr. Greeley that the parish arranged for the installation of the organ prior to the beautiful instrument now in use. At this time, regular meetings were held each month to consider the welfare of the spiritual life in the church. The many absences of the members at the communion service was a distributing factor—as we find it was in the years before. We have seen heretofore that such absentees were summarily treated. Expulsion was the inevitable result, but, this proved an unfortunate antidote. Now such cases were taken care of by urgent suggestion that they realize more seriously their obligations.

The pastor, a thoroughly earnest and conscientious worker evidently felt the strain. An extra four weeks vacation had been voted him, but during the summer of 1866, he felt obliged to give up his work. Finally, on Sept 17, his resignation was regretfully accepted and on the 24th he was formally dismissed by council.

The retiring pastor left a people thoroughly united. We probably might find some delinquents. We know that the debt (somewhat reduced) still existed, but neither fact would deter an earnest working parish from "carrying on." The appreciation for a tireless pastor working for the material and spiritual interests of the church was an outstanding reason for the success of the people.

During the winter of '66 and '67 the pulpit was supplied quite often by professors from the Andover Seminary. The treasurer's book tells us that $15.00 was paid for a "supply." The familiar names of Professors Ropes, Thayer and Mead are often found in the records; also we find the names of several candidates during the early months of '67. In the parish records for April 22, 1867, we had a vote that "the committee who duty it is to supply the pulpit negotiate with Rev. Mr. Flint & Re. Mr. Grassie and ascertain what their services can be obtained for." The latter asked for $1500.00. This was $500.00 more then was paid Mr. Greeley; but the church and parish immediately concurred, and the call was sent him. A unanimous vote "of expression was passed that Rev. T. G. Grassie had all that true piety, love, and devotion to the cause of Christ to become a Pastor of this church and society. His installation occurred Sept. 10, 1867.

—EIGHTEEN—

The new lender was a man well tried in affairs spiritual. A rugged Scotchman from Aberdeenshire, he came as a boy with has parents to this country. Educated at Amherst and Andover, two years service as chaplain in the Civil War, a two years' pastorate in a Maine church; these gave him an experience, which was bound to be for the good in the Methuen church.

He was given a salary of $1500.00. He occupied the house on River Street now owned by Mr. Charles E. Collins. Judging from the country's experience during the aftermath of the World War, we can easily imagine that similar conditions existed at this time in the church's history. Let the easily discouraged this day take courage from the efforts of our forehears. Every part of the organization functioned. There had been a disturbance in the choir; but a few months before the advent of Mr. Grassie, $100.00 was voted "for singing" with the condition "that a committee of three form a choir from our own town." (We believe a good example set their descendants.) At the April meeting (annual) in 1868, the salary was increased to $1600.00 together with the usual vacation of four Sabbaths. $160.00 is voted the choir, including the organist and leader. Nearly $1000.00 was raised by popular subscription. The Ladies Benevolent Society is active in active in raising funds to "place an organ in the church and make alterations in front of the organ as is necessary under the direction of the assessors." At the annual meeting in 1869, the treasurer's report showed that the Ladies Social Circle raised $1053.70 and that the benevolences amounted to $624.10. In 1867, premiums on insurance policies were paid to the amount of $164.00. This covered the organ, meeting house and vestry with its library.

The Covenant, adopted by the church by its founders on Oct. 29, 1729; remained in force for nearly seventy years. The principles of the Westminster Confession had never been a matter of dispute or change. However, the injection of the Half-Way Covenant as well as the danger from the coming of the Socinian views, brought about the adoption of "Symbols of Faith" in 1797 and again in 1816. The Creed adopted in 1816 remained in force for fifty years. In 1869, a mere scriptural statement of belief was adopted. In 1875, a Creed consisting of a mere statement of belief took its place. The establishment of the various churches relieved the rigid adherence to any particular vow. Independency in religious views allowed a freedom not antagonistic to the protestant. The church appears to have dropped the stern Creed of its fathers one hundred Years past, and gone back to the covenant. In 1905, with the by-laws and forms of service" it asks of every member a declaration of a simple covenant which "binds us together as a congregational church". This is the vow taken by us all this day. It includes the covenant of the First Congregational Church of Gainsborough, England drawn up in about 1600.

Possibly an item applicable to our day and generation, is found in the parish records under the date of April 18, 1870. It reads: "A committee that are endeavoring to raise funds to pay the Parish Debt reported that they had succeeded in raising some $4000.00 leaving some $400.00 still wanting to complete the sum necessary." Rev. Mr. Grassie, Deacon Ingalls and Deacon Howe "were appointed to prepare appropriate Resolutions expressive of the feelings of the Parish on t occasion of the payment of the debt of the same." Later the committee arranged to, "having cards distributed in the church for persons to subscribe," a business proposition, no church can be managed otherwise. The appropriations at the May meeting in 1871, were salary and supplies $1565.00; choir $200.00; incidentals $235.00. An echo of a later date is found in a record of 1870 when it was "voted that the assessors be instructed to immediately put the Tower of the church in repair, so as to make it water proof." At this time Miss Helen Simonds, was paid $158.00 for her services as organist and Frank Farr $8.00 for "blowing the organ". A little later the name of M. E. Merrill occurs as organist. In 1871, Daniel Currier choir-leader. Mrs. Longee was paid $28.00 for singing during that year. On April 1, 1872, the debt had to $1028.52. Let us read an few figures in the 1872 report: Preaching $1560.00: interest on $8000 note $56.00; J. O. Parker, insurance $120.00; coal $102.00; J. D. Towle plans for pulpit $40.00; George W. White & Co. Furnace $215.00. The receipts for the year were $2121.67. Sixty-six people subscribed $702.10 in amounts ranging from 50c to $62.40. At this time (May 1872), the debt stood at $00.00 with interest at 7%.

At this time when affairs of the church were prospering and from this distance, harmony seems to have existed throughout the parish, the resignation of Mr. Grassie comes before the people. Two facts are very evident: first that the pastor had brought conditions to an even keel, which made it an opportune time for his release; and second that throughout his letter of resignation there runs a feeling of hesitance as to the fitness of his act.

He emphasized the fact that during his pastorate he had never done any "candidating." His work was here and here he had stayed. Here was his heart. He was not asking for a, release. A church in Wisconsin had sent him an urgent call. It was a field that needed a leader. If the Methuen people could see the need of his going, he would accept the call. He would leave the decision entirely with the church.

A month elapsed. The church decided to let him go. On August 7, 1873, he was dismissed by council. We have dwelt upon this move for the one reason that both pastor and people appear to understand their relative positions that the church possessed a. vitality perhaps not surpassed in its history.

From a local newspaper, the Methuen Gazette of the date July 1, 1873, we cite the following clipping: "We are informed that Rev. Mr. Grassie has resigned the pastorate of the Congregational Society, in anticipation of accepting a like charge over a society in Appleton, Wisconsin. We are exceedingly sorry to hear this, as he has been so long with us here in Methuen, and has entrenched himself so firmly, in the hearts of the people, it will be almost impossible to find his equal in a successor. His departure and absence from the hold of his many years' labor, will cause wide-spread regret. His past associations with parishioners and friends will be reverted to in the years to come, with pleasant remembrances. The society over which he was settled not only loses an able and talented pastor, but our schools, whose management he had to a great extent in charge as chairman of the School Committee, will also be deprived of his earnest and effective work. Methuen is unfortunate in losing and the people of Appleton are fortunate in securing such a citizen and pastor. Our acquaintance with him has been both instructive and pleasant, and our best wishes will follow him to his distant field and labor. It is hoped that he will frequently be enabled to return to us. But more than all, we sincerely wish that he could be induced to reconsider his intention to leave." In passing let us state that Mrs. Grassie is still living-in Eau Claire, Wisconsin.

—NINETEEN—

REV. HORACE LYMAN BLAKE. PARSONAGE PRESENTED BY DEA. J. F. INGALLS. NEW CODE OF RULES.

Speaking again of the material side of our church life, let us state (as we have noticed) that the debt for the time was practically wiped out. We cannot lose sight of such an issue. That the budget for benevolences also was evidently met with a regularity that provoked no outstanding debate, is a situation to be appreciated. More than all this, the records seem to have that smoothness; that lack of interruptions. The various messages of the pastor to his people lack that driving force that he often antagonizes. The coming in and going out of the people lead us to read between the lines the fact that harmony engenders harmony and that whatever the old church really needed it received. Benevolences did not drag. For example: at the annual meeting in 1874 the total amount contributed for benevolences, home and foreign, also local charities amounted to $1388.21. The motive to give was evidently not hampered by the question as to whether it could afford to give. It "cast its bread" with the faith that such would "return" in abundance. It did; with the measure "full and running over."

Such conditions should prepare the way for a worthy successor. We should expect the church to secure a leader. It did. Rev Lyman Horace Blake the pastor in Rowley, Mass. for five years, accepts the call from our people. He was installed on June 25, 1874. The records tell us that the outstanding debt of the church at this time was $1196.00. But the word debt was no deterrent. The parish voted Mr. Blake a salary of $1500.00, four weeks vacation, the use of the parsonage and his moving expenses from Rowley. (The latter amounted to $35.00). At the same meeting, it was voted to raise and appropriate $300.00 to pay for the "parsonage-rent"; $150.00 for the janitor's services, $25.00 for the treasurer's salary and $400.00 for music.

The expression "parsonage-rent" leads us to speak briefly of the second home for residing pastor owned by the church. Our attention is to be turned from the house on River Street above mentioned to the corner of High and Tremont streets where Deacon J. F. Ingalls had recently built a comfortable home. We are told that he felt the need of a suitable parsonage for the church; at the same time he knew that under existing financial conditions it could not bear the additional burden. Located near the church, he rented this to the church. In the following year 1875 "moved by the spirit of God and benevolence, he executed his original intention by deeding the whole property to the parish"; "for the sum of $2400.00." This was "much less than its real value." This gift was at the annual meeting of the parish April 5, 1875. A letter of approval and deep expression of thanks was voted Mr. Ingalls: We quote it complete: Voted to accept Parsonage in accordance with the terms by which it was offered to the Parish; viz: That it should come into the hands of the Parish upon payment by them of $2400.00." The following resolutions were then adopted: "Whereas Deacon Joseph F. Ingalls, a member of the First Congregational Church and Parish, has in a spirit of liberality conveyed to the Parish at a price much less than its real value his land and house thereof known as the parsonage of the Parish; Therefore Resolved that in this transaction which is equivalent to making a gift of considerable value we recognize the fact that we are under lasting obligations for the conveyance upon so liberal terms of a Parsonage which is so nearly adapted to the requirements of the Parish; Resolved that the Parish at its annual meeting, held this Fifth day of April A. D. 1875 approve the arrangement which has been made in relation to the transfer of the Parsonage and accept the same upon the conditions expressed in the deed and also return the thanks of the Parish for so liberal and generous a donation."

The treasurer was instructed, "to give a note of $2400.00 in payment" and $200.00 was appropriated for interest and taxes. The tax on the property for the year 1875 was $35.67. It is of interest to read that for the fiscal year just ending on March 31, 1875, reported by the treasurer at this meeting, an amount of $1971.25 had been subscribed and paid over by eighty-two people.

Two measures were passed during 1874 which may be of interest: it was voted "to dispense with alcoholic wines at communion and hereafter use un-fermented wine." Another matter concerned the old question as to the treatment of members absenting themselves from church service. The reader will recall the method of "excommunication" and later the one of "probation." Now a more moderate method was to be tried. Those dilatory in attendance were to have their names stricken from the roll. It later such should ask for letters of dismission, the same were to be granted.

In June 1875, a "New Code of Rules" was drawn up and accepted. This "Manual" is in our hands today. A note on an early page reads: "For the Larger half of the material in this part of the Manual, the Church are indebted to their former pastor, Rev. Mr. Grassie, by whom it was collected." (Several facts quoted in this history have been taken from this work.) In 1876, we read "that persons ten build horse sheds under direction of the assessors?" During this year a new furnace was installed in the parsonage at a cost of $155.97. The budget, voted at the April meeting in 1877 amounted to $2540.00.

The leadership of Mr. Blake was proving worth while as a successor to that of Mr. Grassie. Both church and parish are in harmony. The older members of the church now living in our midst, tell us of the sincerity with which Mr. Blake worked among hrs people. Strictly pious in his views he appeared to maintain the early tenets of our forefathers and foster the religious fervor of the Calvinist.

But history "repeats itself," just as had happened before, suddenly the resignation of the pastor came before his people. This was on July 7 1877. Like that of Mr. Grassie, it came from a clear sky. "Unsought, unexpected and undesired" are the words used by the resigning pastor. The church was inclined to leave the decision with a council called for that special purpose. In this move, the parish concurred. Such met on Sept. 4, There was nothing to do but grant the request. Mr. Blake went to Boston; pastor of the Vine St. Church and Society.

—TWENTY—

REV. Z. S. HOLBROOK. HIS TROUBLES. REV. J. H. SELDEN. PHILLIPS CHAPEL.

On Oct. 29, 1878, a call was voted Rev. Zephaniah Swift Holbrook of the Oakland Church in Chicago. The exercises of installation were held on Dec. 4. Two former pastors, Blake of Boston and Greeley of Concord, N. H. were members of the council. The latter as moderator; Mr. Blake gave the charge to the people. The new leader coming out of the west, sometimes spoken of as the "breezy vest" where men worked with a rush and hustle; from a center rapidly growing and fast becoming a cosmopolitan center, was destined to find his problems in conservative New England; in a church bound by fixed laws following a man exemplifying the essence of a puritan parish.

Early in the year 1881, there broke out a series of misunderstandings between pastor and people. The records do not tell us of the details. The standing committee had brought charges against the minister. Counter charges came from Mr. Holbrook. We judge simple gossip grew to stories. That these were disturbing to good work was inevitable. There appeared but one way of solution: call a council of the churches of the conference and others round about; not for dismission but for advice and counsel; the list of such to be mutually agreed upon. On Feb. 9, the Council met. Each party was heard. After careful deliberation, the advice given both pastor and people was that both might have been stirred by a simple series of misunderstandings, more or less aggravated by the common talk of the street; yet it is best that a separation occur. It suggests that Mr. Holbrook's usefulness may be reached an end here, though undoubtedly his earnestness and acknowledged abilities can be used in other places. A dissolution between pastor and people was advised, on or before the first of July. On May 22, the resignation was received and accepted by the church. The council for dismission was duly called. It was an extended one. In fact, adjournments continued during the better part of a week before a settlement could be brought about. From June 22 until the 29th charges and specifications were reviewed. Finally on the 29th, the conclusion was reached and commendations with qualifications given either party.

On March 14, 1882, a call was extended to and accepted by Rev. J. H. Selden at a salary of $1300.00 and free use of the parsonage. Also the usual four weeks vacation. Evening services were regularly held each Sabbath. In 1880, a change was made to "hold these on Sunday afternoon at 2 o'clock." We do not read of the success of the move. It appears to have been an echo of the early custom on the "Hill" when the second service was held in the afternoon.

With the reader's permission, we are going to turn aside in our narrative and briefly sketch the history of Phillips Chapel. While such may be familiar reading to many our people, yet to the younger -such may be familiar reading to many of our people, yet to the younger generation many facts should be reviewed. Also, the import of preserving the story directly from the records themselves, make it valuable in itself to coming generations. Here are the facts in words almost as given in the books of the church and parish; On the spot where our chapel of granite now stands, there once stood a plain, wooden structure entirely without ornament. Its dimensions were at first 26 x 50 feet; later enlarged by adding to the rear end. The front and east corner stood nearly as does that of the present building. The date of the erection is not known accurately but we do know that it was built by individuals for the use of the parish. The records show that in March 1837, the Parish is to assume the responsibility of keeping the vestry in repair and pay for the insurance "so long as it is used by said parish." For many years, it was used for prayer meetings and business meetings. A private school was at one time held there; quite often, singing schools. The growth of the town revealed the fact that it was far too small to accommodate the audiences meeting there.

The records tell us that by occupying all the space, two hundred thirty five people entirely filled the building. Such quarters could not meet the demands of a growing center. The Ladies Circle had met in the various homes, which soon became too much a burden upon such homes. We can also imagine that the very appearance of the old building, standing beside the beautiful church of granite, became displeasing to the people. During the pastorate of Mr. Blake, the question of building came up, but the one item of funds seemed to be the deterrent. In the summer of 1880, a certain lady of the parish intimately acquainted with Mr. John C. Phillips, son of a former pastor revealed to him the fact that the ladies of the church were collecting funds for the erection of a new chapel. He immediately offered $1000.00 toward a chapel with the proviso that the erection commence within a year. During the fall and winter, much discussion occurred but nothing definitely done. After the death of Mr. Henry Nevins in March 1881, Mrs. Nevins and sons David and Henry C. gave $3000.00 toward the new chapel in memory of their husband and father. At this time, Mr. Phillips increased his offer to $2000.00 and his mother and sisters gave $400.00 more. The Ladies Circle and the Young Ladies Society had collected $880.00. Now the parish had in its hands $6280.00. At first, nothing was said about a structure of granite and yet the people inwardly felt that such was really needed. These generous donations seemed to allow a building of stone to match the church itself. On June 13, 1881, Daniel W. Tenney, Joel Foster, and Joseph S. Howe were chosen a committee to make arrangements for the immediate commencement of the work. On July 5, the committee reported. The plans of various architects were presented; that of C. W. Damon of Haverhill being accepted. The question of location; whether at the side or rear of the church was a much discussed issue, but finally resulted in the majority favoring the connecting church and chapel as we have it today. On July 12, a building committee of live was appointed to commence the construction of the building: Daniel W. Tenney, Joseph Sidney Howe, Henry C. Nevins, Daniel Currier and James O. Parker. Contract for the stone work was given the lowest bidder, Mr. Moses G. Smith of this town and Parish. On Aug. 22, the old vestry was moved near the street; set up on blocks and made usable until the completion of the new building. The wood work was let to Mr. Jesse A. Towne of this parish. Mr. Daniel H. Rowell had charge of the excavation. The stone-work was completed by the last of November, 1881. During the following winter the house was plastered by S. K. Newell. The woodwork was completed and the painting done by M. W. Keyes. The walls and ceiling were frescoed by Woodland and Casson of Boston. This was early in 1882 The building was completed. Later in the spring, the grounds were graded. The old vestry was moved to a vacant lot near the rail-road station to be used as a mission school conducted by Deacon S. L. Sargent, (M.R. Calvin Taylor was associated with him in the work). This building still stands on Pearl Court as mentioned above).

The new chapel was furnished mainly by the Ladies Social Circle. Mrs. Albert Smith gave a marble clock. Miss E. S. Tenney furnished "the desk for the rostrum." The cost of the chapel including cellar grading and furnishing was about $9500.00. The chapel was named in memory of Rev. John C. Phillips the beloved pastor of this church for twenty years. There was no formal dedication but on June 21, "the members of the church and parish gathered there to meet the generous donors of the Phillips and Nevins families whose contributions had made possible the erection of the building; to thank them for their kindness and in a few simple services of prayer to consecrate the chapel to the worship of God and social fellowship with men." The items of cost are thus recorded: Cellar, stonework and grading about $5000.00; Slating $340.00; Woodwork, painting and windows $2625.00; Fresco work $195.00; Furnishing $900.00; Architect $200.00; Plastering $240.00.

Thus was completed the ideal ever before the minds of a people who for more than a century and a half had been building as they knew. Several church buildings ("meeting houses") had come and gone, but the religious zeal prompting the migration to these shores had borne a fruition that materially would "carry on" for many years. Shall we not look at this work of granite; at this church and chapel and say unto our selves that so shall we "carry on" and "hand down to our children and theirs a message that will continue to a glorious end. Before closing our chapter may we draw the visitor's attention to a large, very common-place looking tablet of wood attached to the wall over the door at the entrance to the chapel. Not a thing of beauty but a joy to the memory of our early fathers. It reads:

"Psalm 84th, 1st Verse. How Amiable are thy Tabernacle O Lord of Hosts! November 3d 1796." A relic of the second meeting-house on the Hill; commemorating its day of dedication.

—TWENTY-ONE—

THE CURRIER-BENSON WOOD LOT.

With renewed energy the two hundred thirty members of the church took up their work under a new pastor and with a purpose borne of the vigor and faith of their ancestors. On Aug. 21, 1883, it was voted to purchase the strip of land north of the horse sheds and south of High Street; thus giving the parish a square piece of land running from Pleasant to High streets. At this same meeting, resolutions of thanks were voted Mr. and Mrs. Joseph Benson Boston for the gift of about fourteen acres of woodland situated in the eastern part of the town. This was at one time a part of the lands of Nathan and Eunice Currier, and passed by will to Mrs. Benson a sister of Mrs. Currier who was for many years a member of this church and had often expressed a desire to give this property to her old church. It was voted that this lot should hereafter be known as the "Currier-Benson Lot." From time to time, the various pastors have taken their winter's supply of wood from this tract. For several years recently, it has been a rendezvous for the various troops of boy scouts.

On April 1, 1884, a vote of thanks was sent Mr. Nevins for his generous offer to move the horse-sheds and provide land for the use of the same. Also at this time came the gift of $5000.00 from the estate of the late Aaron Jacks; to constitute a fund known as the Aaron Jacks Fund, the interest to be used for the "support of the Gospel" in the parish.

In the midst of what appears to have been harmony throughout the church and parish, came the sudden decision of the pastor, Mr. Selden to resign his position. From his letter we judge that for several months he had been unable to do his pulpit work; due to ill health; this was on March 27, 1884. Throughout his words runs a feeling of regret. The loyalty of the parish is keenly appreciated. The standing of the old church in the community is one of leadership, but he feels that he must give way to a man of physical vigor. Thus ended a short pastorate of two years; the shortest in our history.

The membership of the Sunday School has been increased a third. More than twenty additions were made to the church membership; most of them by confession of faith. We read that on Jan. 1, 1884, the roll included the names of two hundred forty people; of which number there were "seventy-three males and one hundred sixty-seven females."

Mr. Selden was formally dismissed by council on May 16, 1884.

At this time in our history, we are to enter upon a pastorate that is to continue for nearly two generations. Twelve pastors had come and gone. During pastorates of different lengths, the First Church had grown strong in its unbroken existence. Men had from time to time left the mother church for others of their choosing. Other churches had been borne; some drawing their vitality from its very side. One through sheer weakness had returned to the fold. Three church homes had been erected. Once was the home as such bodily moved to another section. Pastors are human as, are men everywhere. A few ministers had shown weakness. But, it is the buffeting that begets strength. It is the use of muscles—that makes muscle. At this time, the institution is to be entrusted to one who is to rival the first minister, in length of service; who is to hold his people even as have the strong leaders of the years past.

–TWENTY-TWO–

Rev. Charles H. Oliphant. Finance and Figures. Two benefac-
tors Henry C. Nevins and Edward F. Searles. A third benefac-
tor Mrs. H. C. Nevins. The beautiful Apse. The wonderful La
Farge Window. Improving the neglected burying ground on the
Hill. Kings Daughters.

At a meeting of the church August 19, 1884, the committee with William H. Rogers, Chm. recommended calling Rev. Charles H. Oliphant to the pastorate "as acting pastor for one year." This was the first arrangement of this kind as recorded in our history. The short period of service given by the last pastor together with a willingness on the part of the new minister to serve the year's time as mutual help to either party, seem to explain this new arrangement. The one year proves to be one of satisfaction to church and parish. On July 14, 1885, the unanimous call was extended Mr. Oliphant to be regularly installed pastor. On Oct. 29, just one hundred fifty-six years to a day from that memorable one marking the day when twenty-four men signed their names to a covenant giving birth to this old church; around which was to be built this old town Methuen. Inasmuch as the exercises of installation occurred within the memory of many now living, we may look at the program as arranged for that occasion.

Offertoire in D. Minor   Thayer
Anthem "Send out Thy Light" by the Choir Gounod
Reading records of Council by the Scribe Charles W. Wilcox
Devotional Service led by Rev. C. L. Mitchell
Hymn No. 478
Sermon by Rev. Wm. J. Tucker, D. D.
Solo: "Let Thy Hand Help Me" Mrs. Oliphant
Prayer of Installation Rev. Clark Carter
Charge to the Pastor Rev. J. P. Taylor
Right Hand of Fellowship Rev. Nehemiah Boynton
Address to the People Rev. Owen Street, D. D.
Hymn No. 508

Just a word about the new pastor-elect whose connection with our church is to continue through a space of forty-two years. Couple this pastorate with that of the seventy one years served by the first minister Mr. Sargent (we include the years of "pastor-emeritus" in both cases) and we end that two of the fifteen ministers serving the church during the two centuries were in close touch with the parish for one hundred thirteen years.

Mr. Charles H. Oliphant was the grandson of Rev. David Oliphant, who was graduated from Union College and Andover Theological Seminary. He held past orations in Keene N. H., Beverly and other places in Massachusetts. His grand-mother was the daughter of Dr. Pierson of Andover, "the last of the saddle bag physicians." The father of Charles H. was a merchant in Boston. The son fitted for college at the Schoharie Academy in New York. Illness prevented his entering Williams College as he had planned. He taught at a boys' school in New London, Conn for years. At this time he read law in the office of Judge Alfred Coit, a brother of Rev. John Coit, formerly of Lawrence; passed the examination for the bar. In 1873, he entered Yale Divinity School and was graduated in the class of 1876. His first pastorate was in Orange, N.J. In 1879, he went to Mystic, Conn. and in 1884, accepted the pastorate of our own church here.

At the annual meeting of the parish for this year (1885) held on April 7, the pastor's salary was set at $1500.00 with free use of the parsonage and four weeks vacation. The appropriations were: music $350.00; Taxes $44.00: Interest $300.00; Fuel $125.00; Contingencies $300.00; also voted "to raise a tax of 10% on the valuation of the pews." At this same meeting resolutions were passed on the death of their former pastor the Rev. John C. Phillip. On Sept. 27, 1886, Mr. Henry C. Nevins again becomes a benefactor in contributing toward grading the grounds about the church and arranging for the approaches to the front.

During this year, nearly $800.00 was raised for charity "at home and abroad".

The parish still carries a debt, as formerly, a large part consists of notes held by several members of the church. About six thousand dollars looms up big. But it does not appear to checkmate affairs. $1500 is again agreed upon as the minister's salary. A little later, $300.00 is realized from the sale of wood on the Currier-Benson lot. $400.00 paid for music each year. The members of the choir were chosen from the parish. Their services were paid for, too; the leader as well. $2.00 and $3.00 were amounts paid each Sunday. for certain singers. On April 7, 1890, a request came from the pastor for an increase in his salary. The matter was carefully considered. The people could not see their way to do such. Nevertheless some months later it was voted to grant Mr. Oliphant $500.00 addition to his salary for that year "this not to be taken for a precedent." On Jan. 19, 1892, the church adopted resolutions, "that the thanks of this church he tendered" Mr. Edward F. Searles "for the Pipe Organ presented this day to Phillips Chapel." This organ still stands a memorial to Mr. Searles' generosity; and used at many a service in our chapel.

On Nov. 15, of this same year a special meeting of the parish was called to consider "a proposition of Mrs. H. C. Nevins in regard to improvements of the Church building." The vote was "that the proposal of Mrs. Henry C. Nevins to erect and furnish on the north end of the church building a new apse in memory of her late husband be approved and accepted;" "that the heartfelt thanks of this Parish be extended to Mrs. Nevins for the gift of so fitting an imperishable a monument which will at once enshrine the name of a benefactor and life long friend of said parish while it will add strength and beauty to God's Sanctuary." We must not pass over these lines without gazing with admiration on this beautiful work and agree with the records that the "strength and beauty" is certainly exemplified in this wonderful work, which we trust will endure for many generations.

The work was planned in 1892 and completed about three years later. "The Apse and Window; also the Communion Service are all in memory of Henry C. Nevins of Methuen, a beloved citizen and friend of the Church." "With Mr. John La Farge collaborated his son, Mr. Grant La Farge and Mr. Augustus St. Gaudens, whose designs for the reredos were executed by his brother." The Window acknowledged to be the masterpiece of the artist La Farge is composed of more than ten thousand pieces of glass. The figure of "the Risen Christ" is the central figure. When asked to interpret his wonderful work, the artist replied: "I wished to symbolize or express, or typify the whole idea of the Resurrection, the rising, passing into another life by death, through gloom and darkness, and the clouds of the present, into the less obscured presence of our sole object, God and His light and full satisfaction. It is the expression of a hopeful certitude."

The large apse recesses the pulpit of richly carved old English oak, the lectern, and other pulpit furniture.

On Jan. 17, 1893, it was agreed that the old communion· set be given to the Massachusetts Home Missionary Society in trust for the Swedish Church in Millville, Mass. In the event of the dissolution of that church, to be held by the society aforesaid, for the use of any other worthy church, in their discretion". In April 1894, several meetings were held regarding continuing the practice of the congregation "turning around and facing the choir during the singing of the last hymn at the morning service." Several meetings were necessary to decide the issue. It was voted "not to turn around." At the annual meeting April 9, 1895, it was again voted to allow the pastor an additional $500.00 to his salary "this not be taken as a precedent but in view of the additional subscription pledged for that purpose." At this time, the parish raised $1500.00 for the pastor's salary with $60.00 for supplies during the four Sundays of the usual vacation; $450.00 for music, $175.00 for the janitor's services, $125.00 for fuel and light, $65.00 for taxes, $500.00 for incidentals. $250.00 was paid on the Parish debt. The treasurer's report at this time shows that $100 was realized from the sale of the Mission Chapel. We are not told the name of the purchaser. We understand that today it is the property of the town. It had been rented to the Salvation Army the year previous "under the direction of Bro. F. E. Feilden;" the charge 50c per year. Thus passes, from the church the old building erected in the "thirties," an adjunct to the church moved down from the "Hill." As we have stated above, the reader can now end it on Pearl Court, showing its age but still a memorial to the faithful work of our fathers. The indebtedness of the parish at this time (1895) was $4418.05.

On Dec. 17, 1895, at a meeting of the standing committee resulting from action taken at the last annual meeting regarding "the neglected condition of the burying ground; the matter was taken in hand by some of our good friends and the following motion offered by Dea. Jacob Emerson at the annual town meeting and carried by a unanimous vote: That the town grant to the First Congregational Church of Methuen the privilege of repairing, improving and beautifying, as they may be able, the old Burying Ground and the Common on Meeting House Hill, at the junction of East, Brook, South and Berkeley (formerly Tarbox) Streets, together with the public ground and drives adjoining and to give to the same perpetual care, with the right to make such rules and regulations as shall tend to preserve the old grave stones and monuments from injury and prevent any abuse of the premises without encroaching in any way upon any public rights or any proper use of the same."

It was about this time (1892) that a benevolent organization of the ladies was formed; to be known as "The Phillips Circle of the King's Daughter." The prime movers were Miss Ella P. Bodwell and Mrs. Harry E. Moore (then Miss Edith Johnson.) Twelve names are listed as charter members. The object of the Circle was "to serve others and develop a spiritual growth." The work done; the encouragement given to the sick and shut-in can never be measured. The flowers for the church on each Sunday morning were provided by this society: Christmas cards sent to the aged and countless calls made on those unable to attend church services.

—TWENTY-THREE—

CHURCH FUNDS.

At this time, let us turn aside for a short time from the active movements of church and parish and mention the several funds from which the society draws a steady revenue. The oldest is the so-called Ministerial Fund. This is derived from three sources; (1) from the sale of land and buildings in the easterly part of the town by authority of an Act of the Legislature passed Feb. 24, 1829; (2) from the estate of Thomas O. Poor of Methuen as per his will of April 11, 1850, John Davis, executor; (3) certain accrued interest from John Davis. The fund amounts to about $3500.00.

A second fund the Aaron Jacks so-called has been mentioned above. Mr. Jacks long a member of the parish resided in the west part of the town. By his will dated Dec. 12, 1877, a fund amounting to $5000.00 was left the church in care of three trustees to be chosen by the parish.

A third fund which appears to have been later transferred to the treasury of the parish was created April 13, 1891, when by the wills of Sarah and Harriet N. Merrill certain real estate located at the junction of Charles and Pleasant Streets fell to the first parish. At this time it was voted that such a gratefully accepted and the same constitute a fund known as the Daniel Merrill fund from the name of the father of the donors. This fund consisted of the said real-estate valued at $4000.00 and deposits in three savings banks to the amount of $1850.00. In addition, there were personal notes held against four different parties. On April 1, 1891, the fund in its entirety amounted to $6698.87. During the year 1896, the property in real-estate was sold to Charles H. Tenney for $4000.00. This was turned into the parish treasury and applied on the debt. We find no formal vote regarding this action, but the books tell us of the bank deposits and the notes eventually going into the same channels.

On Apr.11, 1922, the parish voted to sell its parsonage on Tremont street (we shall later tell of this property); thus creating what is known as Parsonage fund. This amounts to about $8000.00.

On Feb. 14, 1922, the parish received $1000.00 from the estate of the late Joseph H. Stone of North Andover, Mass. This fund is known as the Joseph M. and Susan F. Stone Fund in memory of his father and mother "who once worshiped here."

At the April meeting in 1909 we find the first mention of the Thomas O. Poor fund. By the will of said Poor of Methuen, the residue of the estate was to be given to the trustees in charge of the Ministerial fund; the interest from which was to be given to the church to be expended at the discretion of the pastor and committee for the poor needy. The fund is small ($142.40 at the commencement.)

On April 12, 1921 Mr. John D. Emerson, at that time a trustee of both Jacks and Ministerial funds, reported the receipt of $10,000.00 from the estate of the late Charles H. Tenney. With the other trustees he had invested the amount of the fund and turned the proceeds over to the treasurer of the parish. This action was ratified by the society and the Charles H. Tenney fund duly listed with the other funds of the church. The Everett H. Archibald fund was established April 10, 1923. This was a bequest from the estate of the late Everett Archibald for many years an earnest and faithful member of the church. On Aug. 30, the amount $5000.00 was received and in accordance with a vote of the parish put in charge of the trustees for the Jacks fund.

–TWENTY-FOUR–

At the annual parish meeting in 1900 the pastors salary was raised to $1800.00; the same continuing throughout his pastorate. In 1902, Mr. Oliphant's health was so impaired that he was allowed three months' vacation. $180.00 was appropriated to supply the pulpit during that time; this "Instead of our regular $60.00 for supplies."

On April 5, 1904, "voted to proceed on enlargement and improvement of the chapel." The annual meeting 1904 would indicate money borrowed at the bank to the amount of about $1300.00 to meet the cost of extending the chapel and repairing the old part. The report of the building committee in 1905 indicated an expense of $3634.13, of which $434.15 was for repairing the old part.

At the annual meeting in 1906, the question of finances appear to have reached a point when some action should be taken in the way of economy. The meeting was adjourned with a vote that the assessors canvas the parish and see what retrenchments could be made. At this adjourned meeting, the report was made that $600.00 additional had been pledged. $3560.00 was appropriated at this time for the coming year. At a meeting at Deacon Sargent's home. In May, 1902, the resignation of the librarian of the Sunday school was accepted. This may bring to our attention the value of the library in the early years of the church. We are unable ascertain the inception of this factor in our New England institutions. We do know that churches generally maintained this department. Before the writer is a catalogue of the books in the "Library of the First Parish Sabbath

School, Methuen;" it bears the date 1848. The collection numbers 872 books. The field covered is strictly of a religious and moral nature. We might expect a carefully chosen list of this nature. One hundred years ago, the rigid views of the Calvinist had not changed one whit. The stern view of life was as unmovable as the "rock-bound coast itself." In 1907, it was decided to purchase the individual communion set. Judging from a record on July 30, 1907, the regular evening service on Sunday had been faithfully kept. In this report, we read the first break when it was voted "to discontinue the Sunday evening service during July and August." What has proved a lasting movement for the young men and boys of the church found its inception at about this time (1909.)

The naturally inherent "gang" spirit of boys reaching the age of fifteen or seventeen, has often produced the feeling that they are beyond the Sunday School. It is the age when the boy is "betwixt and between". He does not appear prepared for church-membership. An outlet appears to have been found in the secret organization known as X B K. This order with its pin, grip, sign and password so appealed to the boy that its influence has spread even beyond the hopes of the founder. Right here in our own church its inception took place. Mr. Alfred C. Gaunt is the father of the organization. Its religious nature has never been lost sight of. With its social and fraternal tenets it has so grown that today more than seventy chapters with over two thousand members exist in churches of all protestant denominations extending even into the far south. All evidence of the spiritual existing in its ritual is evidenced by the fact that ninety per cent of its members have united with their local church.

On Jan. 4, 1910, at the annual meeting a vote of thanks was given Deacon W. D. Hartshorne "for his very generous installation of an acousticon." On Jan. 25, of this same year, the church granted Mr. Oliphant six weeks' leave of absence that he might return to Clifton Springs for treatment." During his absence, "Dr. Martin will supply the pulpit and attend to the duties of the pastorate." On Oct. 19, 1910, occurred the annual church meeting changed from January in accordance with a vote taken a year since. At this meeting arrangements were made for the twenty-sixth anniversary of Mr. Oliphant's pastorate which would fall on Oct. 29; this also would be the one hundred eighty first anniversary of the founding of the church. Two days, Saturday and Sunday, were given over to this observance. On Saturday, evening a public reception to Mr. and Mrs. Oliphant was held in the church. Several professors from the Andover Theological Seminary were present. Rev. John P. Taylor, D. D. who had given the charge to the pastor at the time of Mr. Oliphant's installation, at this time gave the chief address. On Sunday morning, the pastor gave the anniversary sermon. In connection with this celebration, Miss Alice W. Emerson gave an historical address from the time of the founding of the first Parish to the coming of Mr. Oliphant. An organ recital by Miss Marion B. Emerson "for nearly twenty years the efficient organist of the church" was also a part of the anniversary exercises.

On December 30, 1913, occurred the ordination of Hugh Hartshorne, M.A. PhD. to the Christian ministry. Mr. Hartshorne was the son of our well-known Deacon W. D. Hartshorne recently moved from town but for many years a valued member and worker in our church. The program of the exercises reveals many well-known names. The sermon was preached by Rev. Ambrose Vernon, D. D. of Brookline; the ordination prayer by Prof. W. H. Ryder, D. D. of the Andover Seminary; the charge to the young minister was by his old pastor Mr. Oliphant. Mr. Hartshorne, as far as we can determine by the records, was the fourth young man from our church to enter the ministry; the others being Abijah Cross, Jr., Clarence M. Foss and Arthur V. Fasher.

It is about this time that the double envelope system for pledges with a certain apportionment for benevolences, came into vogue. At the annual meeting in Oct. 1914, an interesting occurrence was noted when the neighboring Baptist church then holding its annual meeting, and this church, entirely unknown to each other, sent messengers with words of good wishes each to the other church. These two, the oldest religious institutions in our town have labored side by side for more than a century.

On April 15, 1917, after a pastorate of nearly thirty-three years. Mr. Oliphant sent his resignation to the church assembled. We quote from the letter: "your need of physical vigor, as for unusual powers of organization and of administration, is insistent. To deprive you longer of the services of a younger man with adequate strength for such exacting work would be an abuse of your loyalty and love." Inter in the season meetings were held at which the resignation was accepted, and Mr. Oliphant elected pastor-emeritus; also a letter-missive to all the churches of the Andover Conference acquainting them with the desire of the Methuen church to defer the formal dismission of their pastor by council until his successor should be chosen at which time the installation of the new pastor and dismission of the old might be arranged "so that one occasion may serve both purposes." At a later meeting, Rev. Frank R. Shipman late pastor of the South Church in Andover was chosen to supply the pulpit until the new leader should be chosen.

On the evening of Oct. 21, a "Recognition Service" for the retiring pastor was given by the Christian League of Methuen. It was largely attended by the people from all the local churches. Ministers from these churches had general charge of the service. It was in 1888, that Mr. Oliphant had conceived the idea of bringing all the churches of the town into united action for the good of the community. With the other three churches then existing, the Baptist Universalist and Methodist, the leadership of our pastor created what was the first league of its kind in America. That this idea had its worth is evidenced by the many formed throughout the country since that time.

The retiring pastor quietly settled in our midst continuing his influence for the best in the church and community. Associated with many departments of town life, his word was often heard in gatherings of local import. For more than nine years, he remained the faithful adviser of both old and young. He passed away on Oct. 7, 1926. He was buried in Walnut Grove Cemetery. He is survived by his wife and three sons. Mrs. Oliphant resides in New London, Conn. We shall hope to have her with us at the Anniversary.

In the World War, the old church stood four-square. Out from its ranks went many a boy and one girl offering themselves as their country might direct. In March 1918, at the suggestion of Mr. Shipman, the acting pastor, a word of greeting was sent to the thirty-two young people in the service. Mr. Oliphant wrote the letter, which was read in church March 10, and copies sent the following week by the clerk.

The following list comprises the names of those in service:

Reginald Remick
Donald Moore
Harrison I Turner
Charles E. Newsholme
Walter Spicer
Dr. Rolf C. Norris
Edward A. Archibald
Frank Harrington
Charles Harrington
Edward B. Douglass
Bernard Webster
Chester Goodwin
Leslie Day
Listen D. Hutchins
David Ferguson
George D. Oliphant
Chester Hutchins
Sidney Cook
Edwin Day
Phillip Crosby
Allen Bailey
Walter Fieldhouse
Russell Foster
Paul Green
Robert Crosby
Merrill Gaunt*

Colby Benson
Frank Learned
David D. Woodbury
Otto R. Wieland
Mary F. Harrington, Red. Cross nurse
*Died

—TWENTY-FIVE—

*REV. PERCY H. EPLER. AN EXCHANGE OF PARSONAGE-PROPERTY, THE
WOMEN AT THE PARISH MEETING. ANOTHER BENEFACTOR MR. ARTHUR
T. WALKER. THE BEAUTIFUL SEARLES ORGAN. THE LOT EAST OF THE
CHURCH.*

On Feb. 22, 1918, after a season of candidating, it was voted
by the church (afterward ratified by the (parish) to extend a call
to Rev. Percy H. Epler of Indianapolis, Ind. to become its pastor. A salary of $1800.00 was given him with the free use of the
parsonize and the usual four weeks' vacation. On Feb. 28, his
letter of acceptance was received. Moving expenses were also
allowed Mr. Epler. The parsonage, now owned by the parish,
was the so-called "Hastings" property on Tremont Street; but a
short distance from the home formerly allowed the resident
pastor. This new house was acquired by an exchange with Mr.
Edward S. Searle. In April 1918, the transfer was formally
arranged. In April 1919, the pastor's salary was increased to
$2500.00. $100.00 was also appropriated for supplies during
the pastor's vacation.

An interesting side-line may be noticed in the various attempts to incorporate church and parish. In 1920, there appeared a concerted effort to bring about the act. This was summarily rejected. At this meeting, a change of minor impor-
tance was brought about. For many year there had existed a
"Board of Censors." This seems to have been a committee to
over-see the affairs of the society; to act as advisors to the assessors; to bring in names of likely members for the society. It
was now (1920) voted to amend the by- laws "that the board of

censors be abolished and that their duties be assumed by the assessors and the clerk." In April 1921, an interesting change in the by-laws is brought about by allowing "the admission of women" to all meetings to have all the voting privileges heretofore confined to the men. At this time the ownership of pews was abolished; that they strike out the words "and owning a pew in the meeting house." At the meeting in April 1922, appear the names of women the first to avail themselves of the privilege of voting in the affairs of the parish. Twenty-one are thus recorded.

During the year just passed the interior of the church was redecorated. The expense was met by an amount raised entirely separate from "the regular collection by the personal efforts of the assessors." At this same meeting in April 1922, "it was unanimously voted to accept the gift of an organ, as offered by Mr. Arthur T. Walker; also "voted that the clerk convey to Mr. Walker the hearty thanks of the parish for this beautiful gift."

The question of repairing the old organ or purchasing a new one had been one long hanging fire. Several attempts had been made to renew the old one. But such had not proven satisfactory; largely through the effort of the clerk of the church, Mr. John Ostler, as well as those of the pastor. Mr. Walker the executor of. and largely the beneficiary from the will or the late Edward F. Searles, gave this beautiful instrument outright to the parish. This organ had at one time graced the mansion of Mr. and Mrs. Searles in Great Barrington, Mass. It had been placed in storage by Mr. Searles with the plan to establish it in a special building for the purpose at Pine Lodge. But the sudden death of Mr. Searles changed all such plans, it was overhauled and rebuilt with electric action. It stands this day one of the largest and most complete organs enclosed in a case that has no superior in the country. It is estimated to be worth at least $50,000.00. This with the Memorial Window valued at $60,000.00, gives the old First Church and Parish an equipment that can not be surpassed in our New England churches; in but few American churches. The organ was dedicated on

October 12, 1924. The cost of installation was about $11,000.00; which amount was entirely met by subscriptions from members of the parish.

The meeting of April 11, 1922, had among other articles to consider, one of special interest in which Mr. Arthur T. Walker again becomes a benefactor. He gives the parish about 46000 feet of bounded by High, Tremont and Pleasant Streets. This gives our church home practically a whole block; all its very own. At this time it was decided to sell the parsonage. It was during this pastorate that Mrs. Sarah Saunders presented the church with the two beautiful gold plates for the communion service.

On Oct. 16, 1923, the resignation of the pastor, the Rev. Percy H. Epler, was read and accepted. On December the council called for the purpose by letters missive, met and formally dismissed Mr. Epler. During the interim to follow, the pulpit was regularly supplied by Mr. Oliphant and Rev. F. D. Hayward. A committee of ten (five from each the church and parish), was chosen to secure the new pastor. On March 2, 1924, Mr. Hayward representing the joint committee presented the name of Rev. Egbert W. A. Jenkinson of Kingston, Rhode Island. The report of the committee was accepted. A letter of acceptance was duly received from Mr. Jenkinson: his pastorate to commence April 21. 1924. The new pastor was voted a salary of $3300.00 with the usual month's vacation. Also $100.00 was allowed him for moving expenses. The parish had sold its parsonage; which now necessitated the pastor seeking his own home. Mr. Jenkinson was formally installed by council on November 12, 1924.

—TWENTY-SIX—

The new pastor was born in London, England. As a boy, he came to this country to live in the far north-west. Later coming east, he lived with his uncle the late Rev. Ruel D. Thomas, D. D. pastor of the Harvard St. Church in Brookline. He was graduated from Tufts College and the Andover Theological Seminary. During The World War, he was engaged in Y. M. C. A. work stationed at Camp Devens. With the vigor of youth he entered upon the work here with a push characteristic of the age. The church of our fathers in their day served its constituents. The institution served its members. Its people came to the meeting house. A neglect of this observance, we have found, often led to dissension. Today the church goes out into the highways and by-ways of life. Our records yellow with age tell us of the men and women of the early years; their activities; their relations. The records this day will tell us of the work and play of the young. The strength of our religious life in the community in years to come will depend largely argon what we give the boy and girl today. We believe the old church is playing an active part in community life. The work with the young is more pronounced. A lover of boy life, Mr. Jenkinson has injected his whole being into this work. The Christian Endeavor society and Sunday School are integral parts of the church life. Two troops of Boy Scouts hold regular meetings in Phillips Chapel. Occasional "hikes" are taken to the "Currier-Benson" wood-lot which has become a rendezvous for the boys. Neither have the girls been neglected. Under the leadership of Miss Florence E. Dodge, a troop of Girl Scouts has been organized.

Let the reader understand however that there have been other activities existing. The present pastor has revived the Men's

Club (defunct more or less) which was created in 1911. The super abundance of social organizations throughout the town would seemingly preclude this "club." However, Mr. Jenkinson has led it through several seasons to make it a part of the social life of the parish.

During the present pastorate, a union of all the societies of the church has been brought about. The Ladies' Society, Missionary Society and King's Daughters have heretofore functioned each for itself as such. That the strength of union be felt, the Phillips Guild, so-called, was organized in the spring season of 1927. Such an organization had before existed, but weakened. The present organization is bearing fruit. All departments are vigorous. Regular meetings following a carefully arranged program have a hearty support from the ladies, throughout the parish.

We have mentioned the community value of the church. Possibly the best illustration may be cited in the Public Forum organized during the first year of the present pastorate. This last March 1929, marks the end of the fifth season. It is an organization nonsectarian. Men from all ranks of life have supported it. Its influence has extended outside the town. From its platform have spoken men and women from every vocation in life. Its inception came from this old church. Not because men in our church have led others to see its value, do we wish it long life; but because we believe that its democratic tenets represent the best interests of a growing church; this we believe the First of Methuen to be.

With the various departments "carrying on;" the Guild, Men's Club, X. B. K., Christian Endeavor, Boys' and Girls' Scout Troops, we can faithfully say that the vitality of the old institution is unimpaired.

The evening service of the church has been abandoned; several years since. The mid-week service has given way to the hurry of modern life with all its engagements. However, for several winter seasons, the pastor has successfully conducted a weekly mid-week session at which books and themes vital to the issues of the day have been discussed with much value to those in attendance.

Thus have we traveled the years measuring the life of the old church and parish. It has been a long journey. Like any trip undertaken it has been impossible to see everything. Two people traveling will never see the same objects. There is not a bit of doubt that we have missed many important scenes. In every work of this nature, there is this inherent weakness. To cover a field of the years is one problem; to cover one of centuries is by all means another. The design has been to make this a history of the old church and parish. We trust the coming generations will End this so to be. As we stated at the commencement, the whole era has been one of changes. The conservatism and fatalism of the Calvinist has given way to the liberal and somewhat lax life of the new ago. But the old church of the eighteenth century still points out the way of life to us of the twentieth. It is still telling men that Heaven's ways are far above those of their own making. Men may come and go; ministers may be called and dismissed, but far above these doings of servants, is the faith of the founders who built that the world might be better. Out from the hearts of such men came this institution. Long may it wave above its head, the flag of truth and righteousness. Long may men endeavor to keep its folds unsullied by the lower acts of life.

THE DEACONS

ELECTED

Robert Swan	Dec. 3, 1729	Died	Dec. 24, 1747
William Gutterson	Dec. 3, 1729	Died	Sept.2, 1742
Joseph Howe	Nov. 30, 1732	Died	Dec. 22, 1771
James Wilson	Nov. 1, 1733	Died	October 20, 1904
Francis Swan	Apr. 1, 1752	Resigned	1755
Ebenezer Barker	1756	Died	Aug. 18, 1805
James Howe, Jr.	Nov. 3, 1764	Died	Jan. 14, 1806
Samuel Cole	1771	unknown	
John Harris	Mar. 25, 1778	Resigned July 11. 1783	
Elijah Sargent	Mar. 25, 1778	Resigned	1789
Josiah Osgood	1783	Died	1788
William Cross	1792	Died	1803
John Huse	Mar. 31, 1796	Died	Sept. 25, 1802
Samuel Webster	Mar. 31, 1796	Died	Apr. 9, 1804
Timothy Emerson	1804	Died	Dec. 4, 1818
William Swan 1806		Died	Apr. 3, 1816
William Bodwell	Jan. 4, 1819	Resigned Aug. 2, 1822	
Thomas Smith	Jan. 4, 1819	Resigned Aug. 1,1831	
Jonas Richardson	May 5, 1823	Died	June 13, 1831
Moses Merrill	Aug. 13, 1831	Died	Apr. 17, 1849
Joseph F. Ingalls	Aug. 13, 1831	Died	Feb. 2, 1876
John Davidson	Jan. 10, 1905	Resigned	Aug. 1, 1867
Edward Carleton	Jan. 10, 1905	Resigned Jan. 30, 1905	

John W. Mann	June 6, 1856	Died	Dec 12, 1861
Joseph Howe	May 16, 1868	Died	Feb. 20, 1895
Samuel G. Sargent	May 16, 1868	Died	Apr. 2, 1906
Edward A. Archibald	May 16, 1868		Sept. 16, 1910
Jacob Emerson, Jr.	1878	Died	May 7, 1907
Charles H. T. Mann	Jan. 7, 1896		Died Aug. 1906
Julian Francis Emerson	Jan. 8, 1901	Died	Dec. 11, 1926
Frank Remick	Jan. 9. 1906	Died	July 18, 1908
William D. Hartshorne	Jan. 8, 1907		
John H. Binns	Jan. 8, 1907	Resigned	March 27, 1905
Elisha B. Homer	Jan. 17, 1908	Died	Feb. 6, 1913
Harry B. Moore	Jan. 5, 1909	Died	Feb. 21, 1921
Caleb A. Page	Jan. 5, 1910	Died	Oct. 28, 1926
Frederick L. Barstow	Oct. 14, 1913	Resigned	Nov. 2, 1915
William Metcalfe	Oct. 14, 1913	Dismissed	Dec. 11, 1927
Edwin L. Haynes	Nov. 2, 1915	Dismissed	Nov. 6, 1926
William H. Buswell	Oct. 18, 1921		
Burton W. Libby	Oct. 25, 1925		
Henry N. Hall	Nov. 1, 1925		
Lewis H. Conant	Oct. 18, 1927		
Frank E. Mitchell	Oct. 18, 1927		

Explanations

P - Profession of Faith

L - United by Letter

H. C. - Received under ""Half-Way Covenant"

Dismissed - by Letter

Dropped - by action of church

Unknown - no data recorded

Excom. - Excommunicated.

The first Twenty-Four Names on a roll were the original covenanters.

a total of 1841 accessions during the two hundred years.

a total of 664 accessions during the firsts century.

Roll of Members

Christopher Sargent		1729	Died	1790
Stephen Barker		1729	Unknown	
John Gutterson		1729	Unknown	
Joseph Morse		1729	Unknown	
Zebediah Barker		1729	Unknown	
Thomas Silver		1729	Unknown	
Evan Jones		1729	Unknown	
Thomas Asten		1729	Unknown	
Benjamin Stevens		1729	Unknown	
James Barker		1729	Unknown	
Ebenezer Barker		1729	Unknown	
Joseph Gutterson		1729	Unknown	
Richard Kelly, Jr.		1729	Dismissed	1740
William Gutterson		1729	Died	1742
John Messer		1729	Unknown	
Abial Kelley, Jr.		1729	Dismissed	1740
John Baily		1729	Dismissed	1740
Samuel Clark		1729	Unknown	
Jonathan Corliss		1729	Unknown	
Isaac Clough		1729	Dismissed	1740
Daniel Peaslee		1729	Dismissed	1742
James How		1729	Died	1771
John Tippets		1729	Unknown	
Robert Swan		1729	Died	1747
Abial Keily, Sr	P.	1729	Dismissed	1740
Mrs. Rebecca Kelly	P.	1729	Dismissed	1740
Richard Messer	P.	1729	Unknown	
James Emery	P.	1729	Dismissed	1742
Stephen Barker, Jr.	P.	1729	Unknown	
James Bodwell	P.	1729	Unknown	
Mrs. Mary Bodwell	P.	1729	Unknown	
Samuel Huse	P.	1729	Unknown	
Mrs. Mary Huse	P.	1729	Unknown	
Elizabeth Barker	P.	1729	Unknown	
Sarah Asten	P.	1729	Dismissed	1740
Mrs. Mariah Barker	P.	1729	Unknown	

Lydia Barker	P.	1729	Unknown	
Mrs. Mehitable Barker	P.	1729	Unknown	
Annis Stevens	P.	1729	Dismissed	1740
Elizabeth Swan	P.	1729	Unknown	
Sarah Swan	P.	1729	Unknown	
Mary Barker	P.	1729	Unknown	
Mrs. Joseph Morse, Sr.	P.	1729	Unknown	
Abigail Morse	P.	1729	Unknown	
Esther Morse	P.	1729	Unknown	
Anne Tippets	P.	1729	Unknown	
Elizabeth Dalton	P.	1729	Unknown	
Mrs. Ruth Gutterson	P.	1729	Unknown	
Sarah Messer	P.	1729	Dismissed	1753
Rebecca Peaslee	P.	1729	Dismissed	1740
Susanna Baily	P.	1729	Dismissed	1740
Mehitable Messer	L.	1729	Unknown	
Ruth Emery	L.	1729	Dismissed	1742
Sarah Clough	L.	1729	Dismissed	1740
Hannah How	L.	1729	Unknown	
Abigail Currier	L.	1729	Dismissed	1740
Mary Silver	L.	1729	Unknown	
Abigail Clark	L.	1729	Unknown	
Elizabeth Corliss	L.	1729	Unknown	
John Gutterson, Jr.	P.	1730	Unknown	
Joseph Morse, Jr.	P.	1730	Unknown	
Mrs. Patience Morse	P.	1730	Unknown	
Zebediah Asten	P.	1730	Unknown	
Mrs. Elizabeth Messer	P.	1730	Unknown	
Mrs. Ruth Kelly	P.	1730	Dismissed	1746
Joanna Gutterson	P.	1730	Unknown	
Nathaniel Messer	P.	1730	Unknown	
William Cross	P.	1730	Died	1803
Mrs. Mary Mirick	P.	1730	Unknown	
John Cross	P.	1730	Unknown	
Mrs. Sarah Cross	P.	1730	Unknown	
Samuel Stevens	P.	1730	Unknown	
Henry Bodwell, Sr.	P.	1730	Unknown	
Jonathan Hartshorn	P.	1730	Unknown	
Mrs. Sarah Hartshorn	P.	1730	Unknown	
James Wilson	L.	1730	Died	1755
Mrs. Martha Wilson	L.	1730	Unknown	

Mrs. Bithia Bodwell	L.	1730	Unknown	
Mrs. Elizabeth Bodwell	L.	1730	Unknown	
James Davis	P.	1731	Unknown	
Meribag Morse	P.	1731	Dismissed	1742
Thomas Eaton	P.	1731	Dismissed	1740
Mrs. Susanna Sargeant	L.	1731	Died	1785
Mrs. Meriam Heath	L.	1731	Unknown	
Mrs. Abigail Messer	L.	1731	Unknown	
Mrs. Henry Bodwell, Sr.	L.	1731	Unknown	
Henry Green	L.	1731	Dismissed	1745
Sarah Corrigal	L.	1731	Dismissed	1736
Mrs. Elizabeth Griffin	L.	1731	Dismissed	1744
Mrs, Sarah Asten	L.	1731	Unknown	
Mrs. Jane Messer	L.	1731	Unknown	
Mrs. Sarah Davis	L.	1731	Unknown	
John Hibbard	L.	1731	Unknown	
Mrs. John Hibbard	L.	1731	Unknown	
Mrs. Dorothy Holt	L.	1731	Dismissed	1740
Mrs. Sarah Gutterson	L.	1731	Unknown	
Joshua Emerson	L.	1731	Dismissed	1740
Mrs. Joshua Emerson	L.	1731	Dismissed	1740
Stephen Merrill	L.	1731	Dismissed	1734
Mrs. Stephen Merrill	L.	1731	Dismissed	1734
Mrs. Mary Whittier	L.	1731	Unknown	
Micah Lancaster	L.	1731	Unknown	
Mrs. Elizabeth Lancaster	L.	1731	Unknown	
Mrs. Lydia Jones	L.	1731	Dismissed	1746
Mrs. Anne Stevens	L.	1731	Unknown	
Mrs. Hannah Lancaster	L.	1732	Unknown	
Mrs. Ebenezer Ayer	L.	1732	Unknown	
William Crummy	P.	1734	Unknown	
Mrs. William Crummy	P.	1734	Unknown	
John Cross, Jr.	P.	1734	Unknown	
Mrs. John Cross, Jr.	P.	1734	Unknown	
Samuel Currier	P.	1734	Dismissed	1740
John Lowell, Jr.	P.	1734	Dismissed	1740
Mrs. Hannah Lowell	P.	1734	Dismissed	1740
Daniel Bodwell	P.	1734	Unknown	
John Ober	P.	1735	Dismissed	1740
James Bodwell	P.	1735	Unknown	
Mrs. James Bodwell	P.	1735	Unknown	

Mary Cross	P.	1735	Unknown	
Hannah Pottles	P.	1735	Unknown	
Mary Barker	L.	1735	Unknown	
Samuel Pottles	L.	1735	Dismissed	1740
Edward Clark	L.	1735	Dismissed	1740
Mrs. Edward Clark	L.	1735	Unknown	
Caleb Richardson	P.	1736	Unknown	
Mrs. Caleb Richardson	P.	1736	Unknown	
James Bodwell, Jr.	P.	1736	Unknown	
Mrs. James Bodwell, Jr.	P.	1736	Unknown	
Susanna Huse	P.	1736	Unknown	
Elizabeth Bodwell	P.	1736	Unknown	
Sarah Emerson	P.	1736	Dismissed	1740
John Hibbard, Jr.	P.	1736	Unknown	
Jonathan Currier	P.	1736	Unknown	
Mrs. Mehitable Barker	P.	1736	Dismissed	1742
Mary Linsey	L.	1736	Unknown	
Sarah Asten	P.	1736	Unknown	
Ebenezer Everett	P.	1736	Dismissed	1742
Abigail Hibbard	P.	1736	Unknown	
Sarah Merrill	P.	1736	Dismissed	1740
Mary Tippets	P.	1736	Unknown	
William Cross, Jr.	P.	1736	Died	1802
Hannah Huse	P.	1736	Dismissed	1730
Widow Whittier	L.	1736	Unknown	
Jonathan Barker	L.	1736	Unknown	
Mrs. Jonathan Barker	L.	1736	Unknown	
Elizabeth Carlton	L.	1736	Unknown	
Katharine Holt	L.	1736	Dismissed	1746
Joseph Stevens	H.C.	1736	Unknown	
Mrs. Joseph Stevens	H.C.	1736	Unknown	
Jonathan Griffin	H.C.	1736	Unknown	
Mrs. Jonathan Griffin	H.C.	1736	Unknown	
Jerusha Tippet	P.	1737	Unknown	
Elizabeth Tippet	P.	1737	Unknown	
William Gage	P.	1737	Unknown	
Mrs. William Gage	P.	1737	Unknown	
Luce Swan	P.	1737	Unknown	
Daniel Gage	P.	1737	Dismissed	1752
Ezra Mirick	P.	1737	Unknown	
Abigail Hastings	P.	1737	Dismissed	1744

Samuel Currier	P.	1737	Unknown	
Martha Hibberd	P.	1737	Unknown	
Mary Merrill	H.C.	1737	Unknown	
Mary Corliss	H.C.	1737	Unknown	
Anne Cross	H.C.	1737	Unknown	
Edward Clark, Jr.	H.C.	1737	Unknown	
Joshua Peaslee	P.	1738	Unknown	
Mrs. Sarah Peaslee	P.	1738	Unknown	
Timothy Mirick	P.	1738	Unknown	
Deliverance Hazeltine	P.	1738	Unknown	
David Dow	P.	1738	Dismissed	1740
Mrs. David Dow	P.	1738	Dismissed	1740
Jerusha Sanders	P.	1738	Unknown	
Sarah Stevens	P.	1738	Dismissed	1740
Mary Emerson	P.	1738	Dismissed	1740
John Baily, Jr.	P.	1738	Dismissed	1740
Mrs Hannah Bailey, Jr.	P.	1738	Dismissed	1740
Richard Skidmore	P.	1738	Unknown	
Thomas Nevens	H.C.	1738	Unknown	
Mrs. Thomas Nevens	H.C.	1738	Unknown	
Judith Harris	H.C.	1738	Unknown	
Oliver Sanders	H.C.	1738	Unknown	
Mary Holt	H.C.	1738	Unknown	
William Sanders	H.C.	1738	Unknown	
Mrs. William Sanders	H.C.	1738	Unknown	
Mary Adams	P.	1739	Unknown	
Ruth Gage	P.	1739	Dismissed	1752
John Harris	P.	1739	Died	1801
Mrs. John Harris	P.	1739	Unknown	
John Mann	H.C.	1739	Unknown	
Mrs. John Mann	H.C.	1739	Unknown	
William Pudney	H.C.	1739	Unknown	
Anne Shoring	H.C.	1739	Unknown	
George Daves	H.C.	1739	Unknown	
Joseph Pudney, Jr.	H.C.	1739	Unknown	
Henry Pudney	H.C.	1739	Unknown	
Hannah Pudney	H.C.	1739	Unknown	
Thomas Asten, Jr.	H.C.	1739	Unknown	
Joshua Emerson, Jr.	H.C.	1739	Dismissed	1740
John Gage	L.	1739	Unknown	
Mrs. Elizabeth Gage	L.	1739	Unknown	

111

Widow Peaslee	L.	1739	Dismissed	1740
Ezra Mirick	L.	1740	Dismissed	1754
Samuel Cross	P.	1740	Unknown	
Timothy Barker	P.	1741	Unknown	
Elizabeth Swan	P.	1741	Unknown	
Abel Merrill	P.	1741	Unknown	
Richard Whittier	P.	1741	Unknown	
Mrs. Richard Whittier	P.	1741	Unknown	
Esther Currier	P.	1741	Unknown	
John Pudney	H.C.	1741	Unknown	
Joseph Pettengill	H.C.	1741	Unknown	
Mrs. Joseph Pettengill	H.C.	1741	Unknown	
John Sprague	P.	1742	Unknown	
William Webber	P.	1742	Unknown	
Abraham Adams	P.	1742	Unknown	
Francis Nicholas, Jr.	P.	1742	Unknown	
Zebediah Barker, Jr.	P.	1742	Unknown	
Job Kimball	P.	1742	Unknown	
Phebe Merrill	P.	1742	Unknown	
Stephen Bodwell	P.	1742	Unknown	
Francis Nicholas	H.C.	1742	Unknown	
Mrs. Francis Nicholas	H.C.	1742	Unknown	
John Merrill	P.	1743	Unknown	
Mrs. John Merrill	P.	1743	Unknown	
William Harvey	P.	1743	Dismissed	1750
Mrs. William Harvey	P.	1743	Dismissed	1750
Robert Thurston	P.	1743	Unknown	
Sarah Davis	P.	1743	Unknown	
Daniel Cross	H.C.	1743	Unknown	
Mrs. Daniel Cross	H.C.	1743	Unknown	
James Maloon	H.C.	1743	Unknown	
James Maloon, Jr.	H.C.	1743	Unknown	
William Maloon	H.C.	1743	Unknown	
Daniel Maloon	H.C.	1743	Unknown	
John. Barker	H.C.	1743	Unknown	
John Linsey	H.C.	1744	Unknown	
Robert Linsey	H.C.	1744	Unknown	
Nathaniel Pettengill	H.C.	1744	Unknown	
Mrs. Nathaniel Pettengill	H.C.	1744	Unknown	
Mrs. Thomas Asten, Jr	H.C.	1744	Unknown	
Hezekiah Asten	P.	1744	Unknown	

Joanna Gilmore	P.	1744	Dismissed	1772
Timothy Swan	P.	1745	Unknown	
Ruth Bodwell	P.	1745	Unknown	
Moses Cross	P.	1745	Unknown	
Judith Asten	P.	1745	Unknown	
Mary Cross	P.	1745	Unknown	
Elizabeth Clark	P.	1746	Unknown	
Sarah Bodwell	P.	1746	Unknown	
Hannah Farnham	P.	1746	Unknown	
Mehitable Wilson	L.	1746	Unknown	
Abigail Bodwell	H.C.	1746	Unknown	
Hannah, Farnham	H.C.	1746	Unknown	
Francis Swan.	P.	1747	Dismissed	1778
Mrs. Lydia Swan	P.	1747	Unknown	
James How, Jr.	P.	1747	Died 1806	
John Parker	L.	1747	Unknown	
Elizabeth Pinney	P.	1748	Unknown	
Aaron Chamberlain	P.	1748	Unknown	
Mrs. Aaron Chamberlain	P.	1748	Unknown	
John Mansur	P.	1748	Unknown	
Mrs. John Mansur	P.	1748	Unknown	
Mrs. Philemon Barker	L.	1748	Dismissed	1761
James Ordway	L.	1748	Unknown	
Caleb Hall	L.	1748	Unknown	
Isaac Asten	H.C.	1748	Unknown	
Nathan Asten	. H.C.	1748	Unknown	
Moses Morse	P.	1749	Unknown	
Mrs. Moses Morse	P.	1749	Unknown	
Samuel Cole	P.	1749	Unknown	
Mrs. Samuel Cole	P.	1749	Unknown	
Moses Pingrey	P.	1749	Unknown	
Mrs. Moses Pingrey	P.	1749	Unknown	
Elizabeth Bodwell	H.C.	1749	Unknown	
Samuel Clark, Jr.	P.	1750	Unknown	
Mrs. Samuel Clark, Jr.	P.	1750	Unknown	
Hannah Sawyer	H.C.	1750	Unknown	
Francis Sawyer	P.	1751	Unknown	
Mrs. Francis Sawyer	P.	1751	Unknown	
John How	P.	1751	Unknown	
Mrs. John How	P.	1751	Unknown	
Hepzibah Hibbert	P.	1751	Unknown	

Jonathan Barker	H.C.	1751	Unknown	
Mrs. Jonathan Barker	H.C.	1751	Unknown	
William Messer	H.C.	1751	Unknown	
Mrs. William Messer	H.C.	1751	Unknown	
James Silver	H.C.	1751	Unknown	
Mrs. James Silver	H.C.	1751	Unknown	
Daniel Silver	H.C.	1751	Unknown	
Mrs. Daniel Silver	H.C.	1751	Unknown	
John Sargent	L.	1752	Unknown	
Mrs. John Sargent	L.	1752	Unknown	
Joseph .Stevens	P.	1752	Unknown	
'Mrs. Joseph Stevens	P.	1752	Unknown	
Abel Huse	P.	1752	Unknown	
Mrs. Abel Huse	P.	1752	Unknown	
Joseph Pettengill	P.	1752	Unknown	
Mrs. Joseph Pettengill	P.	1752	Unknown	
Joseph Sprague	H.C.	1752	Unknown	
Mrs. Joseph Sprague	H.C.	1752	Unknown	
Philemon Barker, Jr.	H.C.	1752	Unknown	
Mrs. Philemon Barker, Jr.	H.C.	1752	Unknown	
Joshua Barker	H.C.	1752	Unknown	
Mrs. Joshua Barker	H.C.	1752	Unknown	
Mrs. Stephen Barker	L.	1753	Died	1776
J Caleb Swan	P.	1753	Unknown	
Mrs. Caleb Swan	P.	1753	Dismissed	1777
Mrs. James Davis	P.	1753	Unknown	
Alice Messer	P.	1753	Unknown	
Nathaniel P. Sargeant	P.	1753	Dismissed	1759
Mercy Perkins	L.	1753	Unknown	
Richard Messer, Jr.	H.C.	1753	Unknown	
Mrs. Richard Messer, Jr.	H.C.	1753	Unknown	
Elizabeth Barker	H.C.	1753	Unknown	
Caleb Sawyer	H.C.	1753	Unknown	
Mrs. Caleb Sawyer	H.C.	1753	Unknown	
John Tippet, Jr.	H.C.	1753	Unknown	
Mrs. John Tippet, Jr.	H.C.	1753	Unknown	
Sarah Parker	P.	1754	Unknown	
Abigail Clark	P.	1754	Unknown	
Hannah Parker	P.	1754	Unknown	
Benjamin Hall	L.	1754	Unknown	
Mrs. Benjamin Hall	L.	1754	Unknown	

Samuel, Parker	L.	1754	Dismissed	1783
Jacob Marston	L.	1754	Unknown	
Mrs. Jacob Marston	L.	1754	Unknown	
John Marston	L.	1754	Unknown	
Mrs. John Marston	L.	1754	Unknown	
Abial Messer, Jr.	H.C.	1754	Unknown	
Mrs. Abial Messer, Jr.	H.C.	1754	Unknown	
Reuben Sawyer	H.C.	1754	Unknown	
Mrs. Reuben Sawyer	H.C.	1754	Unknown	
Joseph Morse, Jr.	H.C.	1754	Unknown	
Mrs. Joseph Morse, Jr.	H.C.	1754	Unknown	
John Pettengill	H.C.	1754	Unknown	
James Russ	P.	1755	Unknown	
William Russ	L.	1755	Unknown	
Mrs. William Russ	L.	1755	Unknown	
Benjamin Morse	H.C.	1755	Unknown	
Mrs. Benjamin Morse	H.C.	1755	Unknown	
Elizabeth Webber	H.C.	1755	Unknown	
Josiah Osgood	P.	1756	Died	1788
Thomas Richardson, Jr.	H.C.	1756	Unknown	
Mrs. Thos Richardson, Jr	H.C.	1756	Unknown	
James Messer	H.C.	1756	Unknown	
Mrs. James Messer	H.C.	1756	Unknown	
Mary Cross	P.	1757	Unknown	
Moses Sargent	P.	1757	Unknown	
Mrs. Moses Sargent	P.	1757	Unknown	
Shsannah Sargent	P.	1757	Unknown	
Benjamin Stevens	P.	1757	Unknown	
Mrs. Benj. Stevens	P.	1757	Unknown	
Benjamin Marston	H.C.	1757	Unknown	
Mrs. Benj. Marston	H.C.	1757	Unknown	
William Morse	H.C.	1757	Unknown	
Mrs. William Morse	H.C.	1757	Unknown	
James Wilson	H.C.	1757	Unknown	
Elizabeth Hall	P.	1758	Unknown	
Samuel Messer	H.C.	1758	Unknown	
Mrs. Samuel Messer	H.C.	1758	Unknown	
Mrs. James Wilson	H.C.	1758	Unknown	
Susanna Lovejoy	P.	1759	Unknown	
Abigail Russ	P.	1759	Unknown	
Anne Davis	P.	1759	Unknown	

Eliphalet Bodwell	H.C.	1759	Unknown	
James Sargent	H.C.	1759	Unknown	
Mrs. James Sargent	H.C.	1759	Unknown	
Moses Barkerr	H.C.	1759	Unknown	
Mrs. Moses Barker	H.C.	1759	Unknown	
Joseph How	P.	1760	Unknown	
Mrs. Joseph How	H.C.	1760	Unknown	
Nathan Abbott	H.C.	1760	Unknown	
John. Grif?n	H.C.	1760	Unknown	
Mrs. John Griffin	H.C.	1760	Unknown	
Mrs. Daniel Williams	H.C.	1760	Unknown	
Henry Bodwell, Jr.	H.C.	1760	Unknown	
Mrs. Hen. Bodwell. Jr.	H.C.	1760	Unknown	
Francis Richardson	H.C.	1761	Unknown	
Mrs. Francis Richardson	H.C.	1761	Unknown	
Anne Herrick	P.	1762	Unknown	
John Page	P.	1762	Dismissed	1763
Mrs. John Swan	P.	1762	Unknown	
Mrs. Jonathan Swan	P.	1762	Unknown	
Joshua Bodwell	H.C.	1762	Unknown	
Mrs. Joshua Bodwell	H.C.	1762	Unknown	
David Austin	H.C.	1762	Unknown	
Mrs. David Austin	H.C.	1762	Unknown	
David Burbank	H.C.	1762	Unknown	
Mrs. David Burbank	H.C.	1762	Unknown	
Ebenezer Carleton	H.C.	1763	Unknown	
Mrs. Eben. Carleton	H.C.	1763	Unknown	
John Davidson	H.C.	1763	Unknown	
John Davidson	H.C.	1763	Unknown	
Daniel Messer	H.C.	1763	Unknown	
Mrs. Daniel Messer	H.C.	1763	Unknown	
Ichabod Perkins	P.	1764	Unknown	
Mrs. Ichabod Perkins	P.	1764	Unknown	
Nehemiah Barker	P.	1764	Unknown	
Mrs. Nehemiah Baker	P.	1764	Unknown	
John Huse	P.	1764	Died	1802
Mrs. John Huse	P.	1764	Unknown	
Daniel Richardson	L.	1764	Unknown	
Mrs. Daniel Richardson	L.	1764	Unknown	
Aaron Gage	L.	1764	Dismissed	1775
Mrs. Aaron Gage	L.	1764	Dismissed	1775

Abner Whittier	L.	1764	Unknown	
Mrs. Abner Whittier	L.	1764	Unknown	
Mrs. Samuel Huse	H.C.	1764	Unknown	
Mrs. James Mailoon	H.C.	1764	Unknown	
Sarnuel Cross	H.C.	1764	Unknown	
Mrs. Samuel Cross	H.C.	1764	Unknown	
Reuben Austin	H.C.	1764	Unknown	
Mrs. Reuben Austin	H.C.	1764	Unknown	
Jacob Messer	H.C.	1764	Unknown	
Mrs. Jacob Messer	H.C.	1764	Unknown	
Ebenezer Barker, Jr.	P.	1765	Unknown	
Mrs. Ebenezer Barker	P.	1765	Unknown	
John Harris	P.	1765	Died	1801
Abial Howe	P.	1765	Unknown	
Mrs. Abial Howe	P.	1765	Unknown	
Dea. Webster	L.	1765	Dismissed	1784
Mrs. Dea. Webster	L.	1765	Dismissed	1784
Mary Bailey	P.	1765	Dismissed	1785
Mrs. Jonathan Baxter	P.	1765	Unknown	
Widow East	P.	1765	Unknown	
Mrs. James Messer	H.C.	1765	Unknown	
Lydia Swan	H.C.	1765	Unknown	
Stephen Messer	H.C.	1765	Unknown	
Mrs. Stephen Messer	H.C.	1765	Unknown	
Hannah Davis	H.C.	1765	Unknown	
Jonathan Baxter	H.C.	1765	Unknown	
Mrs. Asa Cross	H.C.	1765	Unknown	
Mrs. James Cross	H.C.	1765	Unknown	
William Russ, Jr.	H.C.	1765	Unknown	
Mrs. William Russ, J r.	H.C.	1765	Unknown	
Joshua Swan	P.	1766	Unknown	
Mrs. Joshua Swan	P.	1766	Unknown	
Jonathan Currier, Jr.	P.	1766	Dismissed	1774
James Frye	H.C.	1766	Unknown	
Mrs. James Frye	H.C.	1766	Unknown	
Susanna Griffin	H.C.	1766	Unknown	
James Ingalls	L.	1767	Unknown	
Mrs. James Ingalls	L.	1767	Unknown	
Stephen Webster	P.	1767	Dismissed	1784
Mrs. Stephen Webster	P.	1767	Dismissed	1784
David Adams	H.C.	1767	Unknown	

Mrs. David Adams	H.C.	1767	Unknown	
Joseph Griffin	H.C.	1767	Unknown	
Mrs. Joseph Griffin	H.C.	1767	Unknown	
Benjamin Hall, Jr.	H.C.	1767	Unknown	
Mrs. Benj. Hall, Jr.	H.C.	1767	Unknown	
Asa Barker	H.C.	1768	Unknown	
Mrs. Asa Barker	H.C.	1768	Unknown	
Edward Long	H.C.	1769	Unknown	
Mrs. Edward Long	H.C.	1769	Unknown	
Ebenezer Herrick	P.	1770	Unknown	
Mrs. Eben. Herrick	P.	1770	Unknown	
Persis Thom	P.	1770	Unknown	
Rebecca Carleton	P.	1771	Dismissed	1848
Mrs. Kimball Carleton	P.	1771	Unknown	
Esther Sargent	P.	1771	Unknown	
Judith Mirick	H.C.	1771	Unknown	
Daniel Cross	H.C.	1771	Unknown	
Mrs. Daniel Cross	H.C.	1771	Unknown	
Elizabeth Emerson	P.	1772	Dismissed	1784
Mehitable Hazeltine	P.	1772	Unknown	
Martha Hall	P.	1772	Unknown	
Phineas Pettengill	H.C.	1772	Unknown	
Mrs. Phineas Pettengill	H.C.	1772	Unknown	
Elisabeth Baxter	H.C.	1772	Unknown	
Mrs. John Whittier, Sr.	P.	1773	Unknown	
Mrs. Jonathan Barker	P.	1773	Unknown	
Deborah Barker	P.	1773	Unknown	
Dorcas Cross	H.C.	1773	Unknown	
Elijah Sargeant	P.	1774	Unknown	
Mrs. Elijah Sargeant	P.	1774	Unknown	
Benjamin Town	H.C.	1774	Unknown	
Mrs. Benjamin Town	H.C.	1774	Unknown	
Richard Hall	H.C.	1774	Unknown	
Mrs. Richard Hall	H.C.	1774	Unknown	
Judith Cross	H.C.	1774	Unknown	
Phebe Tippet	H.C.	1774	Unknown	
Josiah Gutterson	H.C.	1775	Unknown	
John Sargeant, Jr.	H.C.	1775	Unknown	
Mrs. John Sargeant, Jr.	H.C.	1775	Unknown	
Dorcas Ingalls	P.	1776	Unknown	
Timothy Lovejoy	P.	1776	Unknown	

Mrs. Richard Hall	P.	1776	Unknown	
Enos Parker	H.C.	1776	Unknown	
Levi Parker	H.C.	1776	Unknown	
Mrs. Levi Parker	H.C.	1776	Unknown	
Varnum Hall	H.C.	1776	Unknown	
Mrs. Varnum Hall	H.C.	1776	Unknown	
Thaddeus Gage	H.C.	1777	Unknown	
James Davidson	H.C.	1778	Unknown	
Mrs. James Davidsion	H.C.	1778	Unknown	
Hezekiah Parker	H.C.	1778	Unknown	
Mrs. Hezekiah Parker	H.C.	1778	Unknown	
Peter Marston	H.C.	1779	Unknown	
Mrs. Peter Marston	H.C.	1779	Unknown	
Moses Morse, Jr.	H.C.	1779	Unknown	
Mrs. Moses Morse, Jr.	H.C.	1779	Unknown	
Enoch Parker	H.C.	1779	Unknown	
Mrs. Enoch Parker	H.C.	1779	Unknown	
Francis Swan	P.	1780	Unknown	
Mrs. Francis Swan	P.	1780	Unknown	
Widow Austin	P.	1780	Unknown	
Samuel Webster	H.C.	1781	Unknown	
Mrs. Samuel Webster	H.C.	1781	Unknown	
Aaron Noyes	H.C.	1781	Unknown	
Mrs. Aaron Noyes	H.C.	1781	Unknown	
Mrs. William Whittier	P.	1782	Unknown	
James Ordway, Jr.	H.C.	1782	Unknown	
Mrs. James Ordway, Jr	H.C.	1782	Unknown	
Samuel Marston	H.C.	1782	Unknown	
Mrs. Samuel Marston	H.C.	1782	Unknown	
Jacob Messer	P.	1783	Unknown	
Mrs. Jacob Messer.	P.	1783	Unknown	
Mrs. Rebecca Russ	P.	1783	Unknown	
Susanna Russ	P.	1783	Unknown	
Mary Malston	P.	1783	Unknown	
Mary Marsh	P.	1783	Unknown	
Hannah Poor	P.	1783	Unknown	
Phebe Poor	P.	1783	Unknown	
Mrs. Mary Jennings	P.	1783	Unknown	
Sarah Ingalls	P.	1783	Unknown	
Jacob Tyler	P.	1784	Died	1848
Mrs. Jacob Tyler	P.	1784	Unknown	

Name		Year	Status	Year
John Tippet, Jr.	P.	1784	Unknown	
Mrs. John Tippet, Jr.	P.	1784	Unknown	
Mrs. Hannah Stevens	L.	1784	Unknown	
Abigail Sargent	P.	1786	Unknown	
Simon F. Williams .	L.	1786	Unknown	
Thomas McLeary	P.	1787	Unknown	
Mrs. Thomas McLeary	P.	1787	Unknown	
Timothy Emerson	P.	1787	Died	1818
Mrs. Timothy Emerson	P.	1787	Unknown	
James Sargent	P.	1787	Unknown	
Mrs. James Sargent	P.	1787	Unknown	
Mrs. Mary Bodwell	P.	1787	Unknown	
Molly Swan	P.	1787	Unknown	
Mrs. Sarah Hall	P.	1787	Unknown	
Abigail Springer	P.	1787	Unknown	
Capt. Caleb Swan	P.	1788	Unknown	
John Merrill	P.	1788	Unknown	
Mrs. John Merrill	P.	1788	Unknown	
Robert Hastings	P.	1789	Unknown	
Mrs. Robert Hastings	P.	1789	Unknown	
Samuel Webster	P.	1789	Died	1804
Mrs. Samuel Webster	P.	1789	Unknown	
Jonathan Howe	P.	1789	Unknown	
Mrs. Jonathan Howe	P.	1789	Unknown	
Job Pingree	P.	1790	Unknown	
Mrs. Job Pingree	P.	1790	Unknown	
Elizabeth Emerson	P.	1801	Unknown	
Nancy Huse	P.	1801	Unknown	
Elizabeth Austin	P.	1801	Unknown	
James Davis	P.	1801	Unknown	
Jacob Sargent	P.	1802	Unknown	
Mrs. Jacob Sargent	P.	1802	Unknown	
William Runnels	P.	1802	Unknown	
Mrs. William Runnels	P.	1802	Unknown	
William Swan	P.	1804	Died	1816
Deborah Hibbard	P.	1805	Unknown	
Mrs. Bailey Davis	P.	1805	Dropped	1814
Richard Messer	P.	1805	Dropped	1834
Mrs. Richard Messer	P.	1805	Unknown	
Enoch Poor	P.	1806	Unknown	
Mrs. Prudence Poor	P.	1806	Unknown	

Catharine Currier	P.	1808	Unknown	
Daniel Frye	P.	1808	Dropped	1814
Mrs. Daniel Frye	P.	1808	Dropped	1814
Nathaniel Whittier	P.	1808	Unknown	
Mrs. Nath. Whittier	P.	1808	Unknown	
Mrs. Betsey Currier	P.	1808	Unknown	
Abigail Huse	P.	1808	Unknown	
Mary Sargent	P.	1809 to 1815	Unknown	
Elizabeth Davis	P.	1809 to 1815	Unknown	
Bailey Davis	P.	1809 to 1815	Dropped	1814
Olive Marston	P.	1809 to 1815	Unknown	
Daniel Morse	P.	1809 to 1815	Unknown	
Mrs. Daniel Morse	P.	1809 to 1815	Unknown	
Deborah Carleton	P.	1809 to 1815	Unknown	
Alfred Ingalls	H.C.	1809 to 1815	Unknown	
Joseph Page	H.C.	1809 to 1815	Unknown	
Mrs. Joseph Page	H.C.	1809 to 1815	Dismissed	1828
Ebenezer Hibberd	L.	1809 to 1815	Unknown	
Mrs. Eben. Hibberd	L.	1809 to 1815	Unknown	
John Pettengill		1809 to 1815	Unknown	
Abijah Cross, Jr.	P.	1815	Dismissed	1824
Sarah Poor	P.	1815	Dismissed	1826
Martha Swan	P.	1815	Unknown	
Pamelia Swan	P.	1815	Unknown	
Mrs. Lydia Frye		1816	Died	1854
Mrs. Mary Frye		1816	Unknown	
Mary Carleton		1816	Unknown	
Mrs. Polly Emerson		1816	Unknown	
Mrs. Sally Swan		1816	Unknown	
Samuel Thurlow		1816	Dismissed	1830
Mrs. Samuel Thurlow		1816	Dismissed	1830
Dea. William Bodwell	L.	1817	Died	1824
Dea. Thomas Smith	L.	1818	Died	1836
Mrs. Betsey Smith	L.	1818	Deceased	
Samuel Osgood		1820	Unknown	
Mrs. Abigail Osgood		1820	Unknown	
Enoch Holt		1820	Unknown	
Mrs Rachel Holt		1820	Unknown	
Sally Merrill		1820	Unknown	
John Merrill, Jr.		1820	Unknown	
Joseph A. Bodwell		1820	Unknown	

Fanny Morse		1820	Unknown
Lucy Osgood		1820	Unknown
Sarah Osgood		1820	Unknown
Farnam Hall		1820	Dismissed	1825
William Bodwell, Jr.		1820	Deceased
Jonathan Gardner Davis		1820	Unknown
Mrs. Susanna Davis		1820	Unknown
Mrs. Nancy Kimball		1820	Unknown
Moses Merrill		1820	Died	1843
Mrs. Hannah Merrill		1820	Deceased
Mrs. Mehitable D. Waldo		1820	Dismissed	1831
Dorothy Merrill		1820	Unknown
Martha Stevens		1820	Dismissed	1830
Ebenezer Hibberd, Jr.		1820	Unknown
Samuel Hardy		1820	Unknown
Mrs. Mary Eastman		1820	Unknown
Peter Carleton		1821	Deceased
Martha Clark		1821	Unknown
Jonas Richardson		1822	Died	1831
Mrs. Abigail Richardson		1822	Deceased
Dorcas Carleton		1822	Unknown
Betsey Farnsworth		1822	Unknown
Mrs. Mary How		1822	Unknown
Mrs. Polly Hastings		1822	Died	1857
Abigail Ingalls		1822	Died	1857
Mrs. Phebe Herrick	L.	1823	Dismissed	1868
Stephen Runnels	P.	1823	Unknown
Mrs. Abigail Runnels	P.	1823	Died	1857
Sarah Johnson	L.	1824	Unknown
Hannah Huse	L.	1824	Unknown
Polly Smith	P.	1824	Unknown
Mrs. Persis Messer	P.	1824	Unknown
Mrs. Sally Messer	P.	1824	Died	1870
Caleb Swan	P.	1826	Died	1870
Nathan Currier	P.	1826	Died	1873
Miram Merrill	P.	1827	Deceased
Sena Swan	P.	1827	Deceased
Harriet Farnsworth	P.	1827	Deceased
Joseph F. Ingalls	P.	1827	Died	1876
Washington Merrill	P.	1827	Died	1878

Mrs. Mary (Baily)				
Robinson	P.	1827	Deceased	
John Austin	P.	1827	Dropped	1873
William Frye	P.	1827	Deceased	
Ezekiel T. Abbott	P.	1827	Deceased	
Mrs. Hannah Abbott	P.	1827	Deceased	
Sarah Bodwell	P.	1827	Died	1863
Ruth Bodwell	P.	1827	Deceased	
Mrs. Phebe C. (Frye)				
Ingalls	P.	1827	Died	1876
Mrs. Judith Sawn	P.	1827	Died	1870
Lucy Hall	P.	1827	Deceased	
John C. Eastman	P.	1827	Dismissed	
Phebe Moreland Butrick		1828	Dismissed	1845
Mrs. Francis Bailey		1829	Dismissed	1867
Mrs. Ruth W. Pettengill		1829	Dismissed	1840
Mrs. Persis Wheeler	L.	1830	Dismissed	1843
Sally F. Dustin	L.	1830	Dismissed	
Mrs. Susanna Kelly	L.	1830	Deceased	
Mrs. Prudence Grif?n	L.	1830	Dismissed	1849
Lydia Currier	L.	1830	Dismissed	1842
John T. Sargent		1831	Deceased	
Artemas Herrick		1831	Died	1841
Mrs. Mary Grif?n		1831	Died	1859
Betsey Merrill		1831	Deceased	
Sally Griffin		1831	Deceased	
Hannah Wardwell		1831	Excom.	1837
Dorothy Sargent		1831	Deceased	
Sarah Lowell		1831	Dismissed	1840
Mrs. Mary W. (Balch) Hackett		1831	Dismissed	
Hannah Cochran		1831	Deceased	
Abiah Kelly		1831	Deceased	
Mrs. Saran Kelly		1831	Deceased	
Mrs. Cynthia Hall Hawkes		1831	Dismissed	1840
Elvira Beckwith		1831	Dropped	1875
Hannah Pettengill		1831	Dismissed	
Frederick Messer		1831	Died	1870
Thaddeus Osgood		1831	Dismissed	1840
Tabitha E. Osgood		1831	Died	1833

Benjamin Osgood		1831	Died	1837
Polly Osgood		1831	Deceased	
Olive Morse		1831	Died	1837
Isaac Austin	P.	1832	Deceased	
Mrs. Mary Ann Kimball	P.	1832	Deceased	
Mrs. Mary Frye Hobart	P.	1832	Dismissed	1848
Mrs. Glydia Frye Cross	P.	1832	Died	1853
Louisa Smith	P.	1832	Dismissed	1840
Sally Tyler	P.	1832	Deceased	
John C. Smith	P.	1832	Dismissed	
Joseph How	P.	1832	Died	1895
John Davis	P.	1832	Died	1874
Isaac Morse	P.	1832	Dismissed	1840
Leonard Wheeler	P.	1832	Dismissed	1843
Mrs. Mary Morse	P.	1832	Deceased	
Hannah Griffin	P.	1832	Died	1839
Ruth H. Garland	P.	1832	Dropped	1875
Mrs. Sarah Moore	P.	1832	Dropped	1875
Acsah Hemphill	P.	1832	Dismissed	1854
Lydia Pratt	P.	1832	Excom.	1844
Hannah S. Chamberlain	P.	1832	Dismissed	1838
Mary Grif?n	P.	1832	Deceased	
Sally T. Dudley	P.	1832	Dropped	1836
Sarah Wise	P.	1832	Dropped	1875
Mrs. Abiah Sargent	P.	1832	Excom.	1842
Mary (Schlager) Simms	P.	1832	Died	1877
Mrs. Eunice (Cross)				
Currier	P.	1832	Died	1874
Isaac N. Bodwell	P.	1832	Deceased	
Israel S. Drew	P.	1832	Dismissed	1848
David Hussey	P.	1832	Deceased	1848
Richard Currier	P.	1832	Deceased	
Phebe Eaton O.	P.	1832	Excom.	1841
Mrs. Mary (Wheeler)				
Wilson	P.	1832	Deceased	
Charlotte Sargent	P.	1832	Excom.	
Thomas Grif?n	L.	1833	Dismissed	1847
Mrs. Mary Grif?n	L.	1833	Dismissed	1847
Mrs. Josephine B. Davis	L.	1833	Died	1893
Jane Hemphill	L.	1833	Dismissed	
James Colbert	L.	1833	Dropped	1875

Mrs. James Colbert	L.	1833	Dropped	1875
Clarimond W. Pierce	L.	1833	Dismissed	1840
Mary Lovell	L.	1833	Died	1846
Mrs. Mary Ann (Wilson) Clark	L.	1833	Dismissed	1842
Orrin D. Kimball	P.	1833	Unknown	
Jesse G. Searle	P.	1833	Died	1841
Stephen Huse	P.	1833	Deceased	
Chas. Currier	P.	1833	Dismissed	1843
John White	P.	1833	Excom.	1875
Samuel F. Nichols	P.	1833	Excom.	1840
Thomas Thaxter	P.	1833	Died	1842
Susan Huse	P.	1833	Dismissed	
Mrs. Elizabeth (Pike) Kimball	P.	1833	Deceased	
Mrs. Mary A. Tenney	P.	1833	Died	1837
Mrs. Charlotte P. Huse	P.	1833	Deceased	
Mrs. Sarah F. (Littlefield) Searle	P.	1833	Died	1896
Mrs. Sarah White	P.	1833	Dropped	1875
Mrs. Mary Currier	P.	1833	Died	1839
Mrs. Hannah Nichols	P.	1833	Dismissed	
Mrs. Ruby Thaxter	P.	1833	Died	1843
Mrs. William Carleton	P.	1833	Dismissed	
Mrs. Henry Phelps	P.	1833	Dismissed	
Mlrs. Hannah Messer	P.	1833	Died	1869
Clarissa Marston	P.	1833	Died	1874
Jacob Hull	P.	1833	Deceased	
William Thaxter	P.	1833	Dismissed	1859
Mrs. Hannah Sargent	P.	1833	Deceased	
Rebecca Emerson	P.	1833	Deceased	
Nathaniel Currier	L.	1833	Died	1840
Mrs. Hannah Currier	L.	1833	Died	1873
Mrs. Frances Eaton	L.	1833	Died	1840
Mrs. Mary (Wilson) Towle	L.	1833	Deceased	
John Lowell	P.	1834	Died	1840
Aaron Jacks	P.	1834	Died	1879
Mrs. Mary Jacks	P.	1834	Died	1883
Eliza Bixby	P.	1834	Dismissed	
Asenath Osgood	P.	1834	Died	1858

Susan Osgood	P.	1834	Deceased	
Mary Day Currier	P.	1834	Dismissed	1860
Betsey Alexander	L.	1834	Deceased	
Dorcas I. Davis	L.	1834	Dismissed	
Samuel Eaton	P.	1835	Dismissed	1840
John L. Dudley	P.	1835	Dismissed	
Samuel Hall	P.	1835	Deceased	
Marshall Thaxter	P.	1835	Dismissed	
Henry Spencer	P.	1835	Unknown	
Mary Bowles	P.	1835	Deceased	
Mrs. Polly Hall	P.	1835	Dismissed	1860
Susan Hibberd	P.	1835	Deceased	
Mrs. Eliza J. (Hazeltine) Anderson	P.	1835	Deceased	
Mrs. Jerusha A. (Morse) Getchel	P.	1835	Died	1870
Mrs. Elizabeth E. (Hall) Richards	P.	1835	Dismissed	1839
Mrs. Louisa (Hall) Morse	P.	1835	Dismissed	1875
Isaac Pattee	P.	1835	Dropped	1875
Miriam Bamfeld	P.	1835	Dropped	1875
Jane Morse	P.	1835	Deceased	
Mrs. Betsey (Nutt) Cross	P.	1835	Dismissed	1840
Lavinia S.. Gorrill	L.	1836	Deceased	
Mary Austin	L.	1836	Deceased	
Joseph Pike	L.	1836	Dropped	1875
Mrs. Amanda Pike	L.	1836	Dropped	1875
Edward Carleton	L.	1836	Dismissed	1859
Mrs. Sally Carleton	L.	1836	Dismissed	1859
Mrs. Lucy Sargent	unk	1836	Dismissed	1839
Mrs. L. (Merrill) Smith	unk	1836	Dismissed	1840
Mrs. Robinson How	unk	1836	Excom.	1841
John I. Davidson	L.	1836	Died	1870
Dudley Heath	L.	1836	Died	1840
Achsah. Heath	L.	1836	Dismissed	1841
Matilda Heath	L.	1836	Dismissed	1841
Mrs. Elizabeth Heath Wheeler	L.	1836	Dismissed	1841

Edmond Sargent	L.	1836	Died	1881
Mrs. Betsey Sargent	L.	1836	Died	1875
Mrs. Mary (Sargent) Hibbard	L.	1836	Dismissed	
Caroline Bryant	L.	1836	Dropped	185
Otis Towne	P.	1836	Dismissed	1863
Isabel McCoy	P.	1838	Dismissed	
Mrs. Emily A. Frye	P.	1838	Dismissed	1865
Mrs. Betsey J. (Sargent) Laney	P.	1838	Died	1875
Sarah A. Sargent	P.	1838	Died	1843
Byron Beckwith	L.	1838	Dismissed	1842
John Buckminster	L.	1838	Dismissed	1842
Mrs. Byron Beckwith	L.	1838	Dismissed	1842
Mrs. Francis M. (Wood) Towne	L.	1838	Died	1856
William Thom	P.	1838	Dropped	1875
Mrs. Clarissa C. Smith	P.	1838	Unknown	
Mrs. Mary (McCoy) Fyfield	P.	1838	Dropped	1875
Martha P. Currier	P.	1838	Deceased	
Mrs. Elizaette (Pecker) Hutchins	P.	1838	Deceased	
William Pecker	P.	1838	Dismissed	1860
Betsey C. Towne	P.	1838	Dismissed	1863
A. W. Stearns	P.	1838	Dismissed	
Jeremiah H. Farnsworth	P.	1838	Dismissed	1844
Mrs. Clarinda B. Farnsworth	P.	1838	Dismissed	1844
Elisha J. Carpenter	P.	1838	Deceased	
Mrs. Mary Jane Carpenter	P.	1838	Died	1874
Joseph Smith	P.	1838	Died	1878
Mrs. Harriet Smith	P.	1838	Died	1869
Mrs. Catherine N. Towns	P.	1838	Died	1856
Martha Louisa Putnam	P.	1838	Unknown	
Ruth Bodweil	P.	1838	Deceased	
Mrs Sylvia Taylor	P.	1838	Deceased	
Mrs. Eliza Wheeler	P.	1838	Dismissed	1841
Sarah Hale	P.	1838	Dismissed	

Leverett Swan	P.	1838	Died	1905
Gustavus M. Dole	P.	1838	Died	1839
John C. Drew	P.	1838	Dismissed	1856
Joseph Pecker	P.	1838	Dismissed	
Benjamin Griffn	L.	1838	Dismissed	1819
Albert Smith	L.	1838	Died	1875
Mrs. Lydia Putnam	L.	1838	Deceased	
Mrs. Ann Hale	L.	1838	Died	1858
Mrs. Elizabeth Thaxter	L.	1838	Died	1854
Mrs. Charlotte Hibbaird	P.	1838	Died	1877
Allmira Hibbard	P.	1838	Died	1883
Mrs. Martha J. Sargent	P.	1838	Died	1864
Phebe Ann Herrick	P.	1838	Died	1833
Nancy Frye	P.	1838	Died	1847
Mrs. Abigail B. Baldwin	P.	1838	Deceased	
Lydia Ann Heath	P.	1838	Dismissed	1841
Mrs. Polly Taylor	P.	1838	Died	1889
Mrs. Susan A. Nichols	P.	1838	Deceased	
Elbridge Grif?n	L.	1838	Died	1876
Sarah J. Searle	L.	1838	Died	1895
Adeline Currier	P.	1838	Deceased	
Sarah Currier	P.	1838	Deceased	
William Putnam	L.	1838	Excom.	1841
Enos M. Sweatt	P.	1838	Deceased	
Mrs. Lucretia Robinson	P.	1838	Dismissed	1864
Mrs. Charl?otte Thaxter	P.	1838	Dismissed	
Amos Morse, 2nd.	L.	1838	Deceased	
Perley Morse	L.	1838	Died	1857
Varnurn Tyler	L.	1838	Died	1867
Harris Whittier	L.	1838	Dismissed	1869
Mrs. Hannah B. Jones	L.	1838	Deceased	
Mrs. Mary W. Barker	L.	1838	Dismissed	
Mrs. Lucy C. Morse	L.	1838	Died	1880
Mehitable Doyle	L.	1838	Deceased	
Lewis Young	L.	1839	Dismissed	1843
Mrs. Martha Davidson	L.	1840	Deceased	
Lydia Messer	L.	1840	Dismissed	1856
Ruth Burrill	L.	1840	Dismissed	
Ruby (Ames) Morse		1840	Died	1881
Susan Cole		1840	Dropped	1878
Sabina Joselyn	P.	1841	Deceased	

John H. Strickland	P.	1841	Dismissed	1849
Lucinda Barrett	P.	1841	Dismissed	1848
Enoch Whittier	L.	1841	Died	1881
Mrs. Enoch Whittier	L.	1841	Died	1900
Mrs. Charles Currier	L.	1841	Dismissed	1843
Mrs. Achsah Nevens	P.	1842	Died	1866
Harriet Lake	P.	1842	Deceased	
John Kelsey	P.	1842	Dismissed	1856
Mrs. Mary H. Kelsey	P.	1842	Dismissed	
Hannah Bean	P.	1842	Dismissed	
Joseph Eastman	P.	1842	Dismissed	1861
Osgood Dustin	P.	1842	Dropped	1875
Martha J. Nesmith	P.	1842	Dismissed	1847
Mrs. Mary E. Eastman	P.	1842	Dismissed	1861
Ruth T. Kimball	P.	1842	Deceased	
Laura A. Sanborn	P.	1842	Dismissed	
Charlotte Barker	P.	1842	Dismissed	1866
John Anderson	L.	1842	Died	1857
Mrs. James Durant	L.	1842	Dismissed	
Melinda Burt	L.	1842	Dismissed	
Gilman H. Smith	L.	1843	Died	1899
Mrs. Gilman H. Smith	L.	1843	Died	1894
Mary W. Sargent		1843	Died	1882
Mrs. Hannah Drew		1843	Dismissed	1856
Mrs. Apphia J. (Kimball) Smith	P.	1843	Dismissed	1854
Mary Ann Kelsey	P.	1843 and 1844	Unknown	
Mrs. Mary P. Tenney	P.	1843 and 1844	Dismissed	
Mrs. Maria (Strickland) Ellis	P.	1843 and 1844	Dismissed	1859
John H. Adams	P.	1843 and 1844	Deceased	
Mrs. Joseph How	L.	1843 and 1844	Died	1854
Andrew Styles	P.	1843 and 1844	Dismissed	1877
Mrs. Andrew Styles	L.	1843 and 1844	Deceased	
Mrs. Charlottte Strickland	P.	1843 and 1844	Dismissed	1849
Mrs. Mary H. Smith		1843 and 1844	Dismissed	1854
Nathaniel Whittier	L.	1843 and 1844	Dismissed	1870
Mrs. Mary L. Clay	L.	1843 and 1844	Dismissed	1856
Abbott Jones		1843 and 1844	Deceased	
Mrs. Abbot Jones		1843 and 1844	Deceased	

Name		Year	Status	Year
Mrs. S. G. Adams	L.	1843 and 1844	Deceased	
Susan Adams	L.	1843 and 1844	Dismissed	
Ebenezer Safford	L.	1843 and 1844	Dismissed	1846
Mrs. Marinda Salford	L.	1843 and 1844	Deceased	
Nathan F. Stevens	L.	1845	Dismissed	1847
Mrs. Nathan F. Stevens	L.	1845	Dismissed	1847
Theodore Parsons Huse	P.	1845	Dropped	1877
Mrs. T. P. Huse	P.	1845	deceased	
Henry Knight	L.	1845	Dismissed	1866
Mrs. Henry Knight	L.	1845	Dismissed	1866
Mrs. Susan (Johnson) Jackson	L.	1845	Dismissed	1853
Jerusha Waldo	L.	1846	Died	1861
Abigail Richardson	L.	1846	Dismissed	
Alpheus W. Strickland	P.	1846	Dismissed	1860
Mrs. Mary A. Strickland	P.	1846	Dismissed	
Harriet R. Jones	P.	1847	Dismissed	
Francis Morse	P.	1847	Died	1860
Mrs. Jewett Jones	P.	1847	Died	
Mrs. Hannah Jones	P.	1847	Dismissed	
Dea. John W. Mann	L.	1847	Died	1861
Mrs. John W. Mann	L.	1847	Died	1893
Mrs. Waldo	L.	1847	deceased	
Jacob Tyler, 2nd.	P.	1847	deceased	
Mrs. Susanna Young	L.	1848	deceased	
Mrs. Samuel Sawyer	P.	1849	Dismissed	
Rhoda Guttterson	L.	1849	Probably deceased	
Leonard O. Waldo	L.	1850	Died	1957
Mrs. A. S. Currier	L.	1850	Dismissed	
Eliphalet Kimball	L.	1850	Died	1861
Mrs. Eliphalet Kimball	L.	1850	Died	1869
Mrs. Hannah Baldwin	L.	1850	Died	1850
Isaac H. Laney	L.	1850	Died	1903
Mrs. Lydia E. Merrill	P.	1850	Died	1859
Mrs. Samuel Nichols	P.	1850	Unknown	
Mrs. Caroline Waldo	P.	1850	Died	1858
Hazen W. How	L.	1850	Died	1854
Mrs. Myra J. Bodwell	L.	1850	Deceased	
Phineas How	L.	1850	Died	1879
Mrs. P. How	L.	1850	Unknown	
Mrs. Huldah H. Bodwell	P.	1851	Unknown	

Mrs. H. S. Farrington	P.	1851	Dismissed	1882
Mrs. Ruby Bodwell	P.	1851	Deceased	
Mrs. Martha J. Smith	P.	1851	Died	1900
Mrs. Josephine (Davis)				
Emerson	P.	1851	Died	1911
Alba A. Farr	L.	1852	Died	1906
Samuel S. Mann	P.	1852	Died	1860
Herman Matthews	P.	1852	Dismissed	
William D. Herrick	P.	1852	Dismissed	1868
Moses Merrill	P.	1852	Dismissed	1857
Thomas Thaxter	P.	1852	Dismissed	1852
Jackson How	P.	1852	Died	1862
Mrs. Harriet Buswell	P.	1852	Dismissed	1866
Amanda Buswell	P.	1852	Dismissed	1866
Mrs. Mary H. Mann	P.	1852	deceased	
Henrietta Currier	P.	1852	Dismissed	
Elizabeth H. Smith	P.	1852	Died	1861
George W. Butters	L.	1852	Died	1882
Mrs. George Butters	L.	1852	Died	1879
Martha Butters	P.	1852	Died	1873
Mrs. Amanda Page	P.	1852	Died	1905
Mrs. Susan Bodwell	P.	1852	Died	
Mrs. Harrier A. (Ingalls)				
Sleeper	P.	1852	Deceased	1868
Amanda Swan	P.	1852	Dismissed	1874
Antoinette Pettee	P.	1852	Excom.	1858
Jerusha Waldo	P.	1852	Dismissed	
Mrs. Phineas Smith	P.	1852	Deceased	
Philip S. Severance	P.	1852	Excom.	1860
Adams Cogswell	P.	1852	Dropped	
Robinson H. Bodwell	P.	1852	Deceased	
Mrs. Hannah Dunn	L.	1852	Died	1871
Mrs. Mary A. Morrison	L.	1852	Died	1879
Mrs. Joseph A. Bodwell	P.	1852	Dismissed	1857
George L. Page	P.	1852	Died	1899
Samuel G. Sargent	P.	1852	Died	1906
Mrs. Lovica E. Matthews	P.	1852	Deceased	
Lodiey H. Sargent	P.	1852	Died	1873
Joseph Sidney Howe	P.	1852	Died	1923
Milton G. Howe	P.	1852	Died	1902
Joseph Osgood Bodwell	P.	1852	Deceased	

Prescott Bodwell	P.	1852	Died	1857
Henry L. Knight	P.	1852	Excom.	
Henry L. Currier	P.	1852	deceased	
Phineas Berkley How	P.	1852	Dismissed	
Mrs. P.B. How	L.	1852	Dismissed	
Mrs. Ann M. Hoyt	L.	1852	Died	1880
Mrs. Achsah B. Sanborn	L.	1852	Dismissed	1884
William C. Sleeper	P.	1852	Died	1908
Olivia A. Hoyt	L.	1852	Died	1898
Mrs. Almira M. Kendrick	P.	1852	Dismissed	
Mrs. Almira Kelser	P.	1852	Unknown	
Elizabeth s. Tenney	P.	1853	Died	1895
Ruth Gutterson	P.	1853	Probably deceased	
Mrs. Abigail J. Hall	L.	1853	Died	1865
Osborn Merrill		1853	Dismissed	
Mrs. John Carleton		1854	Died	
Mrs. Sarah a. French	L.	1854	Dismissed	1858
Isaac L. Hibbard	L.	1855	Dismissed	1868
Mrs. I. L. Hibbard	L.	1855	Dismissed	1868
Thomas Carleton	L.	1855	Died	1864
Mrs. Hannah S. Carleton	L.	1855	Died	1892
Mrs. Ira Webster	L.	1855	Unknown	
John K. Merrill	P.	1855	Dismissed	1863
Francis Gage		1855	Died	1859
Mrs. Francis Gage		1855	Died	1863
Mrs. Caroline A. Butterfield		1856	Dismissed	
Mrs. Thomas Webster		1856	Died	1895
Mrs. Mary Ann Tozier	P.	1856	Deceased	
Lydia K. (Kimball) Cross	P.	1857	Died	1917
Mrs. Sarah W. Sargent	L.	1857	Died	1920
Mrs. Eliza Garland Towne	P.	1858	Dismissed	1863
Mrs. Laura Drury	P.	1858	Dismissed	
Mrs. Harriet Churchill	P.	1858	Dismissed	1860
Dolly Lovejoy	P.	1858	Deceased	
James M. Richardson	P.	1858	Died	1901
Mrs. Margaret Richardson	P.	1858	Died	1902
Elizabeth Woodbury	P.	1858	Unknown	

Cecilia Tenney	P.	1858	Dismissed	
Mrs. Susan M. Trow	L.	1858	Dismissed	1868
Mrs. John Smith	P.	1858	Died	1865
Mary Smith	P.	1858	Died	1908
John B. Davidson	P.	1858	Dismissed	1871
Mrs. Francis Davidson	P.	1858	Dismissed	1871
Martha C. Knight	P.	1858	Dismissed	1866
Mrs. Lucy A. (Sargent) Fulton	P.	1858	Died	1924
Arabella L. Churchill	P.	1858	Dismissed	
Susan E. Nichols	P.	1858	Dismissed	1861
Mary Pecker	unk	1858	Dismissed	1861
Mrs. Mary M. Dole	unk	1858	Dismissed	1873
Nelson Hall	P.	1860	deceased	
Mrs. Emeline Hall	P.	1860	Died	1907
Thomas Thaxter	L.	1860	deceased	
Rev. E. H. Greeley	L.	1861	Dismissed	1867
Mrs. E. H. Greeley	L.	1861	Dismissed	1867
Jacob Emerson, Jr.	P.	1861	Died	1907
Johanna A. Knight	P.	1861	Dismissed	1866
Mrs. Rosalia B. Bixby	P.	1861	Dismissed	1869
Sarah S. Hibbard	P.	1861	Dismissed	1868
Samuel Cross	L.	1862	Died	1906
Josephine B. Foote	L.	1862	Died	
Mrs. Mary B. Ayer	L.	1862	Unknown	
Mrs. Harriet Whittier	L.	1862	Died	1888
Mrs. Ellen A. (Merrill) Hardy	P.	1862	Dismissed	1877
Christopher Bodwell	L.	1862	Died	1892
Georgianne (Kimball) Hutchinson	P.	1862	Died	1890
Mrs. S. Augusta Ryder	P.	1862	Dismissed	1866
Mrs. Sarah Jane (Cross) Sleeper	P.	1862	Died	1913
Eliza A. Kimball	P.	1862	Died	1867
Charles Pelham	L.	1863	Died	1876
Mrs. Anna C. Pelham	L.	1863	Died	1876
Catherine C. Webster	L.	1863	Died	1913
Abby S. Mann	P.	1863	Died	1927
Charles Richardson	P.	1863	Died	1888
Mrs. Mary Richardson	P.	1863	Unknown	

Rufus W. Morse	L.	1863	Died	1900
Mrs. Mary C. Morse	L.	1863	Died	1876
J. G. Hubbard	L.	1863	Dismissed	
Mrs. Emily Hubbard	L.	1863	Dismissed	
Amos Webster	P.	1864	Died	1913
Mrs. Judith Butters	P.	1864	Died	1879
Cassandana F.				
(Richardson) Higgins		1864	Died	1904
Adam S. Ballantine		1864	Dismissed	1867
Mrs. Carrie A. Hill	L.	1864	Died	
Edward A. Archibald	L.	1864	Died	1910
Mrs. Addie E.				
Archibald	L.	1864	Died	1885
Mary E. Kittredge	P.	1864	Unknown	
Benjamin Bray	P.	1865	Dismissed	1868
John K. Merrill	L.	1865	Dismissed	1870
Mrs. Mary W. Leach	L.	1865	Died	
Daniel Carleton	L.	1866	Died	1869
Mrs. Martha D.				
Carleton	L.	1866	Died	
Kate B. Sargent	P.	1866	Dismissed	1869
Mrs. Laura A. Barnes	L.	1866	Dismissed	1877
Mrs. Anne M. How	L.	1867	Died	
Rev. Thomas G. Grassie	L.	1867	Dismissed	1872
James S. Dodge	P.	1868	Died	1906
Mrs. J.S. Dodge	L.	1868	Died	
Susie A. Hall	P.	1868	Died	
Leonard Wheeler	L.	1868	Died	1884
Mrs. Persis Wheeler	L.	1868	Died	
Mrs. S. Jane Town	L.	1868	Died	
E. T. Sewell	P.	1868	Died	1868
Mrs. E. T. Sewell	P.	1868	Dismissed	1893
Mrs. Mary Grassie	L.	1868	Dismissed	1873
Mrs. Benjamin Blood	L.	1868	Died	
Mrs. Daniel Merrill	P.	1868	Died	1873
Harriet Merrill	P.	1868	Died	1886
James O. Emerson	P.	1868	Died	1904
Mrs. J. O. Emerson	P.	1868	Died	1914
Mrs. Hannah Dow	P.	1868	Died	1914
Hattie J. Stevens	L.	1869	Died	1925
Nannie (Dow) Smith	P.	1869	Died	1915

134

Mary A. Richardson	P.	1869	Died	1896
Mrs. Leverett Swan	P.	1869	Died	
Mrs. Martha L. Day	L.	1869	Dismissed	1875
Julia A. Kimball	L.	1869	Died	
S. S. Hickok	L.	1869	Dismissed	1881
Mrs. S. S. Hickok	L.	1869	Died	1879
Frank Moore	P.	1869	Dismissed	1873
Rebecca Griffin	P.	1869	Died	1877
Emma F. Peaslee	P.	1870	Dismissed	1878
Joseph L. Shaw	L.	1870	Died	1880
Mrs. Charlotte Shaw	L.	1870	Died	
Sarah M. Moody	P.	1870	Died	
Nathan Smith	L.	1870	Died	1908
Mrs. Nathan (Carleton)				
Smith	L.	1870	Died	1922
Mrs. Ruth L. Everett	L.	1870	Died	1876
Moses G. Smith	P.	1871	Died	1919
Chas. A. Goldsmith	P.	1871	Died	
Mrs. Clara A. Goldsmith	L.	1871	Died	1914
Mrs. Thomas Manning	L.	1871	Died	
Dexter B. Fogg	L.	1871	Died	1887
Mrs. Judith A. Fogg	L.	1871	Died	1921
Mrs. Harriet N. Fogg	L.	1871	Died	1917
Mrs. Annie Sawyer	L.	1871	Dismissed	1872
William Othniel Norris	L.	1871	Died	1920
David Sevey	L.	1871	Dismissed	1872
Minnie Page	P.	1872		
Mrs. Page	P.	1872	Died	1872
Mrs. Catherine				
McCartney	P.	1872	Died	1880
Catherine McCartney	P.	1872	Dismissed	1878
Mrs. Mary (McCartney)				
Mitchell	P.	1872	Died	
Mrs. Mary Beedle	L.	1872	Died	1914
Mary Ellen Beedle	L.	1872	Died	1922
Alonzo Howe	L.	1872	Died	1909
Mrs. Cynthia Howe	L.	1872	Died	1909
Camelia Howe	L.	1872		
Henry Howard Hart	P.	1872	Dismissed	1877
Caroline Scott	P.	1872	deceased	
Mary E. Rogers	L.	1872	Dismissed	1874

Jessie Archibald	L.	1872	Dismissed	1887
William H. Littlebrandt	L.	1873	Died	1906
Mrs. Nancy L.				
Littlebrandt	L.	1873	Died	1904
Samuel Cook	L.	1873	Dismissed	1893
Mrs. Julia Cook	L.	1873	Unknown	
Alonzo P. Chase	L.	1873	Died	1880
Hattie A. (Merrill)				
Chase	L.	1873	Died	1907
Emma A. (Foye) Kent	P.	1873		
Alexander D. Dorward	L.	1874	Dismissed	1880
Joshua Perkins Hill	P.	1874	Deceased	
Sarah E. Wyman	P.	1874	Unknown	
Martha Emma Welch	P.	1874	Deceased	
Rosilla Libby	P.	1874	Dismissed	1875
Elizabeth H. Merrill	P.	1874	Died	1899
Mrs. Lucy Maria (Hall)				
Page	P.	1874	Died	1888
Geo. W. Newell	L.	1874	Died	1885
Mrs. M. L. Newell	L.	1874	Died	1899
Mrs. Susan R. Grif?n	L.	1874	Died	
Mary Frances Farr				
Dearborn	L.	1874	Died	
Lyman H. Blake	L.	1874	Dismissed	1877
Mrs. Isabella T.				
(Mather) Blake	L.	1874	Dismissed	1877
Mary Eva Littlebrandt				
Dorward	P.	1875		
Fannie E. (Sewall)				
Warren	P.	1875	Dismissed	1888
Henry L. Knight	Rest.	1875	Dismissed	1875
Donald McDonald	L.	1875	Dismissed	1875
Mrs. Donald McDonald	L.	1875	Dismissed	1878
Mrs. R. L. Elder	L.	1875	Dismissed	1878
Susie A. Page	P.	1875		
Sarah M. (Bodwell)				
Davis	P.	1875	Dismissed	1922
Emma A. (Bodwell)				
Hutchins	P.	1875	Dismissed	1922
Mrs. Alice E. (Harris)				
Gutterson	P.	1875	Died	1913

Mrs. Helen F. (Parker)				
Spooner	P.	1875	Dismissed	1878
Mrs. Frances C. Parker	P.	1875	Died	1916
James O. Parker	P.	1875	Died	1910
Vvilliam Merrill Rogers	P.	1875	Died	1919
Maggie C. (Farr) Kelley	P.	1875	Dismissed	1880
Carrie C. (Emerson)				
Fisher	P.	1875	Dismissed	1890
Ella H. (Towne)				
Webster	P.	1875	Died	1910
Hattie L. (Archibald)				
Wardwell	P.	1875		
Addie C. Sargent	P.	1875	Died	
Sarah L. (Sargent)				
McGonagle	P.	1875	Dismissed	1887
Mary A. Crosby	P.	1875	Dismissed	1883
Mrs. Mary (Tenney)				
Howe	P.	1875	Died	1905
Mrs. Caroline A. (How)				
Rogers	P.	1875	Died	1919
Mrs. Eunice Fulton	L.	1875	Died	
Lydia Fulton	L.	1875	Died	1906
Mary Fulton	L.	1875	Dismissed	1879
Charles J. Fulton	L.	1875	deceased	
Mrs. Martha J. Crosby	L.	1875	Dismissed	1883
Addie F. Crosby	L.	1875	Dismissed	1888
Richard Irvin	L.	1875	Dismissed	1904
Mrs. Sarah Irvin	L.	1875	Dismissed	1904
Henry Laverty	L.	1875	Dismissed	1877
Mrs. Christina Laverty	L.	1875	Dismissed	1877
Daniel Merrill	L.	1875	Died	1878
Sarah Merrill	P.	1875	Died	1888
Charles T. Masterson	P.	1875	Dismissed	1876
Mrs. Wilson T.				
Masterson	P.	1875	Dismissed	1876
Lizzie (Wheeler) Newell	P.	1875	Deceased	
Ella. P. Bodwell	P.	1875		1928
Mrs. Sarah Spicer	L.	1875		1876
Mrs. Nancy J. Wilson	L.	1875	Deceased	1875
Margaret Jennie Wilson	L.	1875	Died	1876
Aaron Everett	L.	1875	Died	1878

Mrs. Mary E. Everett	L.	1875	Died	1875
Isabella. A. Marden	L.	1875	Dismissed	1876
Robert L. Elder	P.	1876	Dismissed	1878
Henry N. Hall	P.	1876		
Mrs. Mary F. Hall	P.	1876		
Charles W. Mann	P.	1876		
Charles Jackson	P.	1876	Dismissed	1899
Mrs. Sarah A. Jackson	P.	1876	Died	1896
Ada (Jackson) (Norris)	P.	1876	Died	1883
James Spicer	P.	1876	Died	1927
J. Francis Emerson	P.	1876	Died	1926
Mrs. Harriet I. Emerson	P.	1876	Died	1992
A. Laburton Emerson	P.	1876	Died	1910
Carrie H. Grosvenor	P.	1876	Died	1979
Mrs. Eliza. J. Trow	P.	1876	Died	
Mrs. Abbie E. Nowns	P.	1876	Dismissed	1879
Eliza. Merrill	P.	1876	Died	1913
Everett H. Archibald	P.	1876	Died	1915
Elisha B. Homer	P.	1876	Died	1898
Mrs. Sarah E. Homer	P.	1876	Died	1918
Mrs. Alice Craig	P.	1876	Unknown	
Mrs. Augusta A. Foye	P.	1876	Died	1908
Samuel Webster	P.	1876	Died	1886
Emma L. (Webster)				
Merrill	P.	1876	Died	1913
Nancy H. Kimball	P.	1876	Died	1915
Mrs. Janette C. Noyes	P.	1876	Died	1898
Calvin J. Sargent	P.	1876	Died	1918
Mrs. Mary A. Sargent	P.	1876	Died	1920
Mrs. Fanny M. Webster	P.	1876	Unknown	
James C. Taylor	P.	1876	Died	1908
Mrs. Sarah Taylor	P.	1876		
Clara E. (Caswell)				
Slack	P.	1876	Unknown	
Emma B. (Chase)				
(Murray)	P.	1876	Died	1881
Fannie H. (Merrill)				
Frederick	P.	1876	Died	1911
Hattie G. (Sargent)				
Copp	P.	1876	Dismissed	1884
Mary M. Bowen	P.	1876	Died	1905

Joseph W. Fulton	P.	1876	Died	1930
Annie Taylor	P.	1876	Unknown	
Jennie E. Hardy	P.	1876	Dismissed	
Charles M. Howe	P.	1876	Dismissed	1913
Robert Moffatt	P.	1876	Died	1915
Samuel Huse	L.	1876	Died	1889
Mrs. Elizabeth E. Huse	L.	1876	Died	1895
Lizzie F. Huse	L.	1876	Died	1925
Mrs. Sarah M. Webster	L.	1876	Died	
Mrs. Clara J. Gorman	L.	1876	Dismissed	1887
Mrs. Sarah B. Sawyer	L.	1876	Died	1927
Mrs. Louisa M. Fuller	P.	1876	Unknown	
Katie I. (Sleeper) Pierce	P.	1876	Dismissed	1888
Elizabeth Trow Trask	P.	1876	Dismissed	1881
Georgiette A. Fogg	P.	1876	Died	
Hannah Bushnell	P.	1876	Unknown	
Mrs. Ann Janeth Stevens	P.	1876	Died	1919
John Manderson	P.	1876	Dismissed	1899
Mrs. Joanna Manderson	P.	1876	Died	1787
Charles E . Trow	P.	1877	Dismissed	
Mary (Mann) Ball	P.	1877	Dismissed	
Mrs. Ruth Kent	L.	1877	Died	1879
Thomas Cunningham	P.	1877	Died	1873
Frank E. Jackson	P.	1877	Dismissed	1899
Albert V. Fisher	P.	1877	Dismissed	1896
Edward Farr	P.	1877	Died	1886
George M. Kelley	P.	1877	Dismissed	
George W. Barrett	P.	1877	Unknown	
J. Liston Emerson	P.	1877	Died	1898
Frank J. Ball	P.	1877	Dismissed	1878
Mrs. Mary B. Quimby	P.	1877	Unknown	
Charlotte E. (Smith) Doble	P.	1877	Dismissed	1913
Benjamin Blood	P.	1877	Died	1879
James P. Blood	P.	1877	Died	1881
Frank W. Strickland	P.	1877	Dismissed	
Frank B. Pierce	P.	1877	Dismissed	1886
Owen Copp	P.	1877	Dismissed	1884
Benjamin Gonnam	P.	1877		
Alfred J. Foster	P.	1877	Dismissed	1909
Minnie P. Tutwiler	P.	1877	Unknown	
Stella E. (Kelley) Foster	P.	1877	Died	1893

Minnie L. Holt	P.	1877	Dismissed	1879
Robert Jamieson	P.	1877	Died	1907
Helen H. Jamieson	P.	1877	Died	1916
Mrs. Mary McFarland	P.	1877	Unknown	
Mrs. Emma O. Pierce	P.	1877	Died	1902
William R. Patterson	P.	1877	Dismissed	1878
James McFarland	P.	1877	Dropped	1880
Frederic A. Spear	P.	1877	Dismissed	1883
Mrs. Laura A. Spear	P.	1877	Dismissed	1883
Mrs. Henrietta A. Hibbard	L.	1877		
Mrs. Elizabeth C. Bingham	L.	1877	Dismissed	1878
Charles H. T. Mann	L.	1877	Died	1906
Jesse Ayer	P.	1877	Died	1880
Mrs. Margaret A. Carlton	P.	1877	Died	1995
George F. Carlton	P.	unk	Dismissed	1899
Mrs. Abigail Blood		unk	Died	1882
Mrs. Leonard Wheeler		unk	Died	1882
Capt. Cunningham	P.	1879	Died	1878
Alice Emerson	P.	1880		
Fred Roscoe Caswell		unk	Died	
Mrs. John Davis		unk	Died	1893
Mrs. Margaret Griffin		unk	Died	1898
Miss Mary A. Higgins		unk	Dismissed	
Eliza Bixby		unk	Dismissed	1898
Mrs. Cyrus Wilson		unk	Died	1877
Mrs. Hazen Bodwell		unk	Dismissed	1878
Mrs. Mary M. Ball		unk	Dismissed	1878
Mrs. Henrietta E. Currier		unk	Died	1887
Miss Mary O. Carleton		unk	Died	1887
Miss Sarah Merrill		unk	Died	1888
Mrs. Fannie E. (Sewell) Warren		unk	Dismissed	1888
Mrs. Robert R. Taylor.		unk	Died	1889
Mrs. Harriet (Crosby) Hutchins		unk	Died	1890
Mrs. Albert Smith		unk	Died	1899
Mrs. Leach			Died	1882
Mrs. Charles Richardson			Died	1888
Miss Louie M. Stevens			Died	1889
Mrs. G. W. Jones			Dismissed	1890

Mrs. Harriet Hutchins			Died	1890
Mrs. Daniel Carleton			Died	1890
Mrs. Georgianna Hutchinson			Died	1890
Mrs. Samuel Rowe			Died	1883
Mrs. James Fulton			Died	1892
Mrs. Harriet White Graven			Dismissed	1893
Clara J. Gonnam			Dismissed	1887
Mary E. Sargent			Dismissed	1887
D. A. White			Dismissed	1884
Mrs. John C. Webster			Died	1883
Mrs. Rebecca Gustin			Died	1885
Mrs. Edward A. Archibald			Died	1885
Mrs. Lizzie W. Newell			Dismissed	1880
Miss H. B. Trask			Dismissed	1881
Mrs. Mary F. Dearborn			Dismissed	1881
Fred T. Caswell			Dismissed	1882
Eliza Craig			Dismissed	1882
Mrs. Betsey J. Laney			Died	1882
Henry Spenser			Died	1882
Mrs. Joseph Howe			Died	1882
Mrs. Louisa Merrill	L.	1877	Unknown	
Josie E. (Merrill) Dyer	L.	1877	Dismissed	1894
George N. Barnard	L.	1877	Died	1905
Rev. Z. S. Holbrook	L.	1879	Dismissed	1886
Mrs. Z. S. Holbrook	L.	1879	Dismissed	1886
Mrs. Mary C. Austin	L.	1879	Died	1919
Rufus W. Morse	L.	1879	Died	1900
Mrs. Mary C. Morse	L.	1879	Dismissed	1903
Selwin A.. Dodge	L.	1879	Dismissed	1908
A. E. Rollins	L.	1879	Died	
Charles Rockwood	L.	1879	Died	
Mrs. Julia A. Rockwood	L.	1879	Died	
Mrs. Ida Stevens	P.	1879		
Daniel A. White	P.	1880	Died	
Charles L. Mitchell	P.	1880	Dismissed	1890
Mrs. Charles L. Mitchell	L.	1880	Dismissed	1890
Mrs. .Mary G. Emerson	L.	1880	Died	1893
Rev. J. H. Selden	L.	1882	Dismissed	1884
Mary E. Sargent	L.	1883	Died	1887
Mary L. Stevens	L.	1883	Died	1928
Katharine F. Crocker	L.	1883	Dismissed	1919

Jennie A. (Archibald)				
Emerson	L.	1883	Died	1924
Thomas Pearson	L.	1883	Dismissed	1886
Helen M. (Barnard)				
Lowell	L.	1883		
Matilda E. Roberts	L.	1883	Dismissed	1887
Perley E. Goodhue	L.	1883	Dismissed	1886
T. W. H. Hussey	L.	1883	Dismissed	1894
Mrs. Gertrude Hussey	L.	1883	Dismissed	1894
Mrs. Ella Coffin	L.	1883	Dismissed	1889
Mrs. Eliza J. Anderson		unk	Died	1896
Mrs. Elvira B. Jones		unk	Died	1896
Mrs. Catherine L. Morse		unk	Dismissed	1898
Thaddeus C. Foster		unk	Died	1901
Mrs. Sarah (Swan) Leverett		unk	Died	1902
Mrs. Marion (Coe) Kelley		unk	Dismissed	1903
Mrs. Hulda Jane Towne		unk	Died	1905
Mrs. Lucy B. Stevens		unk	Died	1905
Mrs. Mary A. Webster		unk	Died	1906
Mrs. Sarah M. Webster		unk	Died	1906
Mrs. Amelia Manning		unk	Died	1907
Mrs. Lucy W. Gile		unk	Died	1908
Mrs. Sarah M. Bodwell		unk	Died	1921
Mrs. John Hall		unk	Dismissed	1918
Mrs. Eveyh S. Dodge		unk	Died	1913
Sarah M. Moody		unk	Died	1921
L. Webster Silver		unk	Died	1921
Mrs. Russell Spring		unk	Dismissed	1921
Caroline B. Morse		unk	Died	1922
Mrs. Mary E. Crowell		unk	Died	1923
Mrs. Almeda Dudley Call		unk	Dismissed	1914
Mrs. Isabel Skinner		unk	Dismissed	1916
Mrs. M. L. Bailey		unk	Dismissed	1876
Harriet Chamberlain	L.	1883	Dismissed	1902
Grace K. (Webster)				
Holman	L.	1883		
Grace E. (Stevens)				
Woodard	L.	1883	Dismissed	1887
Leona W. (Foster)				
Taylor	L.	1883	Dismissed	1899
Caroline A. Smith	L.	1883	Unknown	

Fred M. Page	L.	1883	Died	1919
Rev. Charles H. Oliphant	L.	1884	Died	1926
Mrs. Charles H. Oliphant	L.	1884		
Jacob Kessler	L.	1885	Dismissed	1887
Mrs. Emma Archibald	L.	1885	Died	1909
Fannie Gohman	L.	1885	Unknown	
Mrs. Daniel Shipley	L.	1885	Unknown	
Mrs. Sarah. C. Norris	L.	1885	Died	1922
Wilbur Shipley	L.	1885	Dismissed	1899
Mrs. Lucy B. Stevens	L.	1885	Died	1895
Mary (Smith) Waud	L.	1885	Dismissed	1909
Kate (Smith) Morse	L.	1885	Dismissed	
Mrs. Mary A. Higgins	L.	1886	Dismissed	1893
Mrs. Isabel Skinner	L.	1886	Dismissed	
Mrs. Louisa Kessler	L.	1886	Dismissed	1886
Mrs. C. E. Chickering	L.	1886	Died	1903
Mrs. Sarah Emsley	L.	1886	Dismissed	1895
Mrs. Augusta M. Archibald	L.	1886	Died	1926
Lucinda Greenwood	L.	1886	Died	1901
Margaret White	L.	1886	Dismissed	1892
Joseph Emsley	L.	1886	Dismissed	1893
A. L. Emerson	L.	1886	Dismissed	1898
H. T. Chickering	L.	1886	Died	1890
Annie B. (Homer) Emerson	P.	1886	Dismissed	1900
Effie Kessler	P.	1886	Unknown	
Isabella H. (Morse) Lang	P.	1886	Dismissed	1903
J. Liston Davis	P.	1886	Died	1889
Rev. Samuel Rowe	P.	1886	Dismissed	1895
Sophronia Rowe	L.	1886	Unknown	
Isaac Wyatt	L.	1886	Unknown	
Minnie Jamieson	P.	1886		
Charlotte C. (Swan) Lyons	P.	1886	Dismissed	1904
Bessie M. Swan	P.	1886	Dismissed	
Eliza C. Mitchell	P.	1886	Dismissed	1890
Frank Remick	L.	1886	Died	1908
Mrs. Fannie Remick	L.	1886	Died	1922
Mrs. Ida Austin	L.	1886		

Mrs. Julia Russell	P.	1886	Died	1922
Mrs. Alice M. (Russell)				
Foster	P.	1886		
Marion B. Emerson	P.	1886		
Alice G. (Foster) Mann	P.	1886	Died	1898
Frank H. Dunmore	L.	1886	Dismissed	1888
Mrs. Kate R. Dunmore	L.	1887	Dismissed	1888
Andrew Watts	L.	1887	Dismissed	1899
Mrs. Annie Watts	P.	1887	Unknown	
George W. Archibald	P.	1887		
Charles P. Emerson	P.	1887	Dismissed	
J. Maude (Archibald)				
Buswell	P.	1887		
L. Maude (Irving)				
McAllister	P.	1887	Dismissed	
John J. Bunker	P.	1887	Died	1907
Mrs. Minnie E. Bunker	P.	1887	Dismissed	1911
Mertina Goldsmith	P.	1887	Dismissed	
Charles O. Goldsmith	P.	1887	Dismissed	1899
Maude H. Fernald	P.	1887		
Elizabeth J. Howe	P.	1887	Died	1925
Annie J. Whittier	P.	1887		
Maude A. (Rollins)				
Robinson	P.	1889	Dismissed	1908
Asenath I. (Sawyer)				
Welton	P.	1889	Dismissed	1893
Georgia I-I. (Emerson)				
Puffer.	P.	1889	Dismissed	
Annie F. Archibald	P.	1889	Died	1909
Mrs. Annie Hull	P.	1889	Died	1906
Mrs. Clara Carleton	P.	1889	Died	1915
Mrs. Addie Fogg	P.	1889		
William T. Fernald	P.	1889	Died	1923
Charles B. Chandler	P.	1889	Dismissed	1890
Bessie C. (Sargent)				
(Woodbury)	P.	1889	Dismissed	1911
Maude J. (Marble)				
Johnson	P.	1889	Dismissed	1919
Mrs. Susan R. Grif?n	P.	1890	Died	1895
William H. Buswell	P.	1890		
Edward D. Taylor	P.	1890	Dismissed	1899

144

Thaddeus C. Foster	P.	1890	Died	
Harry E. Moore	P.	1890	Died	1921
Mrs. Rebecca N. Whittier	P.	1890	Died	1926
Martha J. (Whittier) Downing	P.	1890		
Mrs. Sarah Marble	L.	1890		
Frank A. Fielden	L.	1891	Dismissed	1902
Mrs. Margaret H. Fielden	L.	1891	Dismissed	1902
Mrs. Stephen D. Crowell	L.	1891	Died	1910
Mrs. Mary E. Johnson	L.	1891	Died	1901
Mrs. L. R. Gilmore	L.	1891	Died	1915
Mrs. Lucy W. Gile	L.	1891	Died	1908
M. Edith (Johnson) Moore	L.	1891	Dismissed	1925
John Ostler	P.	1891		
Charles B. Marble	P.	1891	Dismissed	1918
Daniel H. Sawyer	P.	1891	Died	1912
Horace Carleton	P.	1892	Died	1899
Stephen D. Crowell	P.	1892	Died	1910
Lillie M. (Cushing) Plummer	P.	1892	Dismissed	1894
Ellen McCrerry	P.	1892	Dismissed	1902
Jennie P. Driscoll	P.	1892	Dismissed	1892
Margaret L. Fielden	P.	1892	Dismissed	1903
Ardella C. Crowell	P.	1892		
Catharine F. (McGuire) Drown	P.	1893		
Martha L. (Sargent) Dow	P.	1893		
Mrs. Frances M. Hardy	P.	1893	Dismissed	1896
Edna A. (Skinner) Marsh	P.	1893	Dismissed	1915
Ella Louise (Skinner) Whi'te	P.	1893	Dismissed	
Marion Coe	P.	1893	Dismissed	1898
Blanche (Hall) Berwick	P.	1893		
Mrs. Helen Spooner	L.	1894	Died	1917
Mrs. Abbie S. Parker	L.	1894	Dismissed	1893
A. O. Blake	L.	1894	Dismissed	1902

Name		Year	Status	Year	
Mrs. Anna K. Moffatt	L.	1895			
Joseph A. Bailey	L.	1895			
Mrs. Joseph A. Bailey	L.	1895			
Mrs. Harriet E.					
Woodbury	L.	1895	Died	1826	
Alzada M. Tenney	L.	1895	Died	1919	
Caleb A. Page	L.	1895	Died	1926	
Henry Gaunt	P.	1895	Died	1906	
Mrs. Mary L. Gaunt	P.	1895			
Eva M. (Weir) Warden	P.	1895	Dismissed	1887	
James Gaunt	L.	1895	Dismissed	1900	
Mrs. James Gaunt	L.	1895	Dismissed	1900	
Alfred C. Gaunt	L.	1895			
George Albert Marsh	L.	1895	Died	1925	
Mrs. George A Marsh	L.	1895			
E. C. Frost	L.	1895	Died	1897	
Mrs. E. C. Frost	L.	1895	Dismissed	1898	
Carrie E. Frost	L.	1895	Dismissed	1901	
Mary A. Frost	L.	1895	Dismissed	1898	
James F. Frost	L.	1895	Dismissed	1898	
Milan Anderson	L.	1895	Died	1900	
Mrs. Milan Anderson	L.	1895	Died	1914	
William Eldon	L.	1895	Dismissed	1899	
Mrs William Eldon	P.	1895	Dismissed	1899	
Martha J. Highton	P.	1895	Dismissed	1899	
Mrs. Irene R. Patterson	P.	1896	Dismissed	1907	
Mrs. Nancy B. Douglass	P.	1896			
Helen R. Jamieson	P.	1896	Dismissed	1922	
Orrin E. Follansbee	L.	1896	Dismissed	1899	
Mrs. Mary A. Follansbee	L.	1896	Dismissed	1899	
Nettie M. Follansbee	L.	1896	Dismissed	1899	
Amanda M. Reed	L.	1896	Died	1918	
Samuel Eleazor Mann	L.	1896	Died	1922	
Mrs. Emily E. Davis	L.	1896	Died	1908	
Mrs. Mary E. Hunt	L.	1896	Died	1919	
Harriet A. Sleeper	P.	1897	Dismissed	1918	
Fzinnie G. Spicer	P.	1897			
Helen G. (Foster)					
Payson	P.	1897			
Jesse B. Shirley	L.	1897	Died	1921	
Mrs. Jesse B. Shirley	L.	1897	Died	1922	

Name		Year	Status	Year
May S. (Shirley)				
Thacher	L.	1897	Dismissed	1916
Mrs. Isabella				
MacFarlane	L.	1897	Died	1907
Catherine Macfarlane	L.	1897		
Isabel Macfarlane	L.	1897	Dismissed	1922
Jean Macfarlane	L.	1897	Dismissed	1922
Mrs. Hattie B.				
Williamson	P.	1897	Died	1902
D. Annie (Hill) Davis	P.	1897		
Lewis G. Alexander	L.	1897	Dismissed	1898
John Ferguson	L.	1897	Dismissed	1902
Mrs. Emily S. Gillette	L.	1897	Dismissed	1902
Theron E. Fisher	P.	1897	Dismissed	1900
Annie R. Spicer	P.	1897		
Clara H. Coburn	L.	1897	Dismissed	1915
Mrs. Lewis G. Alexander	L.	1897	Dismissed	1898
Mrs. John Ferguson	L.	1897	Dismissed	1903
Federick R. Knott	L.	1898	Died	1922
Mrs. Frederick R. Knott	L.	1898	Died	1904
Alexander D. Mackenzie	L.	1899	Dismissed	1908
Mrs. Alex. D. Mackenzie	L.	1899	Dismissed	1908
J. Varnum Coburn	L.	1899	Dismissed	1917
Mrs. J. Varnum				
Coburn	L.	1899	Dismissed	1917
Mrs. Clara (Gillette)				
Stephens	L.	1897	Dismissed	1902
Arthur J. Crosby	P.	1900		
Elsie C. Hartshorne	L.	1900		1912
Mrs. Lucy A. Crosby	L.	1900	Died	1913
Mrs. Elizabeth K. Morse	L.	1899	Died	1914
Elizabeth G. Morse	L.	1899		
Alfred Newsholme	L.	1899	Died	1905
Nettie M. Clark	P.	1899	Dismissed	1922
Anna B. (Morse)				
Mitchell	P.	1899		
Mrs. Alfred Newsholme	L.	1899	Died	1915
Josephine Beard	L.	1899	Dismissed	1890
R. Johnson Brooks	L.	1900	Dismissed	1901
Mrs. M. Elizabeth				
Brooks	L.	1900	Dismissed	1901

Name		Year	Status	Year
William Patton	P.	1900	Died	1904
Mrs. William Patton	L.	1900	Died	1923
William D. Hartshorne	P.	1901		
Mrs. William D.				
Hartshorne	L.	1901		
Andrew T. Jackson	P.	1901	Dismissed	
Mrs. Andrew T. Jackson	L.	1901	Dismissed	
Mrs. Bernice B. Burley	L.	1901		
Ethel Mary (Irving)				
Hudson	P.	1901	Dismissed	1904
George W. Oliphant	P.	1901		
Ernest Henry Gaunt	P.	1901		
Isaac Hartshorne	P.	1901	Dismissed	1911
Hugh Hartshorne	P.	1901	Dismissed	1914
Mrs. William Morris	L.	1900	Dismissed	1910
Mrs-. Betsy K. High	L.	1901		
Mrs. Fannie G. Coe	L.	1902	Dismissed	1896
'William Metcalfe	L.	1902	Dismissed	1927
Mrs. William Metcalfe	L.	1902	Died	1919
Mary E. Bailey	P.	1902	Died	1923
Florence E. Dodge	P.	1902		
Helen M. Fogg	P.	1902		
Bertha A. Jowett	P.	1902		
Mary E. Newsholme	P.	1902		
Ruth Norris	P.	1902		
Mabel A. (Page)				
Delphy	P.	1902	Dismissed	1929
Beatrice (Spicer)				
Feather	P.	1902	Dismissed	1916
Mrs. Albelta E.				
(Irish) Davie	L.	1902	Dismissed	1911
Maude A. Irish	L.	1902		
John F. Tenney	L.	1902	Dismissed	1906
William K. Ephlin	L.	1903	Dismissed	1923
Mrs. Helena M. Ephlin	L.	1903	Dismissed	1923
Margaret Ferguson	P.	1903	Dismissed	1903
Anna (Ferguson)				
Gibson	P.	1903	Dismissed	1918
Nelson E. Gaunt	P.	1903	Died	1903
Mrs. Helen M.				
(Spooner) Spring	P.	1903	Dismissed	

F. Harley Remick	P.	1904		
Leroy H. Irish	P.	1904	Dismissed	1923
Sidney A- Cook	P.	1904	Dismissed	
Jennie C. Robinson	P.	1904	Unknown	
Almeda F. (Harrington) Call	P.	1904	Died	1921
Ethel Marian Dorward	P.	1904		
Irving M. Archibald	P.	1904		
Harold L. Irish	L.	1904	Dismissed	1922
Edward M. Lowell	P.	1904		
Paul Green	P.	1904	Dismissed	1922
Edward B. Douglass	P.	1904		
Reginald W. Remick	P.	1904		
John H. Binns	L.	1904		
Mrs. Florence A. Rafferty	L.	1904		
Mrs. Philomena C. Cook	L.	1904		
Rolf C. Norris	L.	1904		
Frank Binns	P.	1905	Dismissed	1918
Anna Remick	P.	1905		
Rev. Charles A. Breck	L.	1905	Dismissed	1911
Mrs. Mary M. Breck	L.	1905	Dismissed	1911
John Parr, M. D.	L.	1905	Dismissed	1926
Agnes Fraser, M. D.	L.	1905		
Caroline B. Morse	L.	1905	Died	1923
Mrs. Clara (Cook) Arnold	L.	1905	Dismissed	
Blanche (Silver) Hunter	P.	1905	Dismissed	1922
John Tyler Douglass	P.	1905		
Elizabeth (Jowett) Archibald	P.	1905		
Elliot P. Spooner	P.	1905	Died	1927
Walter Spicer	P.	1905		
Charles C. Fisher	L.	1905		
Mrs. Charles C. Fisher	L.	1905		
Edith Goldsmith	P.	1905		
John F. Lacey	L.	1905	Dismissed	1912
Mrs. John F. Lacey	L.	1905	Dismissed	1912

Name	Type	Year	Status	Year
Janet M. G. (Cuthill)				
Wilson	L.	1906	Dismissed	1922
Marian (Cuthill)				
Greenwood	P.	1906		
Merrill S. Gaunt	P.	1906	Died	1916
Frederick L. Barstow	P.	1907	Dismissed	1917
Mrs. Beula L. Barstow	P.	1907	Dismissed	1917
Mrs. Vera G. Chisholm	P.	1907	Dismissed	
Helen R. (Frederick)				
Horton	P.	1907	Dismissed	1911
Marietta Jowett	P.	1907		
Florence E. (Page)				
Haycock	P.	1907	Dismissed	1915
Lillian F. (Learned) Scott	P.	1907		
Mrs. Bessie A. Gordon	P.	1907	Dismissed	1909
Emma R. Pfeiffer	P.	1907		
Alma F. (Pfeiffer)				
Eastwood	P.	1907	Dismissed	1915
Arthur D'. Murray	L.	1907	Dismissed	1912
Dorothy Binns	P.	1907	Died	1910
Mrs. Mary (Gordon)				
Barrett	P.	1907		
William Dawson	L.	1907	Dismissed	1922
Mrs. Jane Ellen				
Dawson	L.	1907	Dismissed	1922
Alexander D.				
McDonald	P.	1907	Dismissed	1910
John Chamley	L.	1908	Dismissed	1913
Mrs. John Chamley	L.	1908	Dismissed	1913
Mrs. Sarah Hail	P.	1908		
John Ferguson	L.	1908	Dismissed	1918
Mrs. John Ferguson	L.	1908	Dismissed	1918
Emma (Ferguson)				
Henderson	L.	1908	Dismissed	1914
Annie' Ferguson	L.	1908	Unknown	
John Eastwood	L.	1908	Dismissed	1915
Frederick W. Gay	L.	1909		
Mrs. Frederick W. Gay	L.	1909		
Aroline Goodwin	P.	1909		
Nellie Southworth	P.	1909		

Name		Year	Status	Year
Mary (Harrington)				
Tennien	P.	1909	Dismissed	1922
Leslie B. Day	P.	1910	Dismissed	1922
David Ferguson	P.	1910		
Beatrice F. Herrick	L.	1910		
Helen A. (Rafferty)				
Taylor	P.	1910		
Mary M. (High) Ware	P.	1910		
Mrs. Agnes McDonald	L.	1910	Dismissed	1915
Isabella McDonald	L.	1910	Dismissed	1915
Mary McDonald	L.	1910	Dismissed	1915
Helen (Emmons) Reoch	P.	1910		
Prank Douglass	P.	1910		
Mrs. Miriam H. Bennick	P.	1910	Dismissed	1914
Adelaide (Stevens) Kay	P.	1911		
Mrs. Elizabeth Morton	L.	1911	Dismissed	1917
A. H. James	P.	1911	Died	1914
Edward Archibald	P.	1911		
Frank Learned	P.	1911		
Donald J. Moore	P.	1911	Dismissed	1923
Harvey S. Gruver	L.	1911	Dismissed	1912
Mrs. Mary K. Gruver	L.	1911	Dismissed	1912
Arthur Kemp	L.	1911		
Mrs. Arthur Kemp	L.	1911		
Mrs. Sarah E. Saunders	L.	1912	Died	1923
Mrs. Fannie I. Bennett	P.	1912	Dismissed	1922
Clara A. Bennett	P.	1912	Dismissed	1922
Eber W. Ephlin	P.	1912	Dismissed	1922
Sydney C. Metcalfe	P.	1912		
Frank E. Mitchell	L.	1912		
Fred Buzzell	P.	1912	Dismissed	1922
Harold E. Bailey	P.	1912		
Archibald M. Dodge	P.	1912	Dismissed	1913
Annie A. Barnes	L.	1912	Dismissed	1926
Edwin L. Haynes	L.	1913	Dismissed	1926
Mrs. Edwin L. Haynes	L.	1913	Dismissed	1926
Edna F. (Haynes)				
Bartlett	L.	1913		
Beth G. (Haynes)				
Heald	L.	1913	Dismissed	1917
Harry Bennett	P.	1913	Dismissed	1922

Mrs. Helen Barker	P.	1914	Died	1921
Alice M. Merrill	P.	1914	Dismissed	1929
Rev. Ernest C. Davis	L.	1914	Died 1920	
Mrs. Letitia. E. Kendall	L.	1914		
Ruth Archibald Buswell	P.	1914		
Edith Irene (Benson) Gardner	P.	1914	Dismissed	1916
Mrs. Annie P. Wieland	P.	1914		
Alice R. (Mann) Russell	P.	1915		
James J. Simpson	L.	1914	Dismissed	1917
Florence E. Kemp	P.	1915		
Charlotte (Mikalson) Gast	P.	1915		
Mrs. Hannah C. Holt	P.	1915	Dismissed	
Mrs. Alfred C. Gaunt	L.	1915		
Russell J. Footer	P.	1915		
Mildred A. (Foster) Woodln	P.	1915		
Mildred L. (Ostler) Johnson	P.	1915	Dismissed	1925
Marlon E. (Ostler) Whitehead	P.	1915		
Katherine W. Reed	P.	1915	Dismissed	1919
Colby H. Benson	P.	1915	Dismissed	1916
Walter D. Lowell	P.	1915		
Percy G. Hook	L.	1915		
Mrs. Percy G. Hook	L.	1915		
Gordon F. Hook	L.	1915		
Warren E. Stowers	P.	1915	Dismissed	1918
Henry L. Barstow	P.	1915	Dismissed	1918
Gertrude L. Hemenway	P.	1915	Died	1919
Sigrid H. (Mikalson) Mitchell	P.	1916	Dismissed	1929
Mrs. John Tyler Douglas	P.	1916		
Mrs. Margaret J. White	P.	1916		
Mrs. Martha. A. Tewksbury	L.	1916		
Robert Mason	L.	1916	Dismissed	1922
Edward C. Marden	P.	1916	Died	1917
Wilfred A. Kemp	P.	1916		

Marlon J. (Crosby)				
Jenkins	P.	1916		
Mary E. (Mann)				
Bradstreet	P.	1916		
Ruth D. Morrison	P.	1916		
Mildred F. (Webster)				
Harrington	P.	1916	Dismissed	1917
David Anderson	L.	1916		
Mrs. Elizabeth M.				
Blodgett	P.	1917		
Elsie R. (Ostler)				
Johnson	P.	1917		
Clifton F. Swain	P.	1917		
Jessie H. (Robinson)				
Lowell	P.	1917		
Reynold G. High	P.	1917		
Ernest K. High	P.	1917		
Ruth C. (Haynen)				
Pendexter	P.	1917		
Arthur M. Stevens	L.	1917		
Mrs. Arthur M. Steven	L.	1917		
Otto R. Wieland	P.	1917		
Mrs. Martha. E. Duncan	P.	1917		
Cindy B. (High)				
Ferguson	P.	1917		
Donald H. Scott	P.	1917		
Harold D. Oliphant	L.	1917		
Mrs. Harold D.				
Oliphant	P.	1917	Dismissed	1919
Mrs. Maud H. Mackey	P.	1918	Dismissed	1919
Beatrice Wood	P.	1918	Died	1920
Clarence White	P.	1918		
Herbert Craven	P.	1918		
Rev. Percy H. Epler	L.	1919		
Mrs. Percy H. Epler	L.	1919		
Palmer Epler	L.	1919		
Albert Rawnsley	L.	1919	Dismissed	1922
Mrs. Albert Rawnsley	L.	1919	Dismissed	1922
Mrs. Claire R. Goodwin	L.	1919	Dismissed	1926
Mrs. Edith C. Scott	L.	1919		
Burton W. Libbey	L.	1919		

Roy V. Baketel, M. D.	P.	1919		
Mrs. Roy V. Bekelzel	P.	1919		
Sherman Beketel	P.	1919		
John Beketel	P.	1919		
Lawrence Byrne	P.	1919	Died	1926
Thomas Byrne	P.	1919		
Dorothy Q. (Davis)				
Noring	P.	1919		
Helen G. Devil	P.	1919		
Frank Duncan	P.	1919		
Helen D. Foster	P.	1919		
Martin F. Goodwin	P.	1919	Dismissed	1926
Matthew Harrison	P.	1919		
Mrs. Matthew Harrison	P.	1919		
James E. Hayne	P.	1919		
Lorena. K. Harlow	P.	1919		
Chesley Hastings	P.	1919		
Walter M. Hastings	P.	1919		
Walter M. Hastings, Jr.	P.	1919		
William E. Heald	P.	1919		
Mrs. Sarah C. Hutchins	P.	1919	Died	1921
Marian H. (Hutchins)				
Tripp	P.	1919		
Roy Hook	P.	1919		
Ruth W. Hook	P.	1919		
Howard Lowell	P.	1919		
Norman Lowell	P.	1919		
Gabriel H. Malootian	P.	1919		
Amelia M. (Mitchell)				
Howe	P.	1919		
Grace E. (Mitchell)				
Birch	P.	1919		
Maurice E. Ordway	P.	1919		
Edward Vernon 'Reed	P.	1919		
Mrs. Caroline M.				
Silloway	P.	1919		
James W. Stott	P.	1919		
David D. Woodbury	P.	1919	Died	1926
Mrs. David D.				
Woodbury	P.	1919		
Robert A. S. Reoch	L.	1919		

Margaret H. Colburn	L.	1919		
Mrs. Everett H. Archibald	L.	1920		
Rev. Frederick D. Hayward	L.	1920		
Mrs. Frederick D. Hayward	L.	1920		
Helen Epler	P.	1920		
Roland B. Hutchins	P.	1920		
Helene E. (Johnson) Jackway	P.	1920		
Albert McPherson	P.	1920		
Donald A. Pettee	P.	1920		
Leverett N. Putnam	L.	1920		
Mrs. Leverett N. Putnam	P.	1920		
Marcella Tamey	P.	1920		
Arthur W. Templeman	P.	1920		
F. Delmont Tootell	P.	1920		
Doris (Wood), Speed	P.	1920		
Clara S. (Batcheller) Marble	L.	1920		
Arthur Atkinson	P.	1920		
Beth Swain	P.	1920		
Mrs. Rowena Swain	P.	1920		
Charles E. Marsh	L.	1920		
Mrs. Charles E. Marsh	L.	1920		
John M. Park	L.	1920		
Mrs John M. Park	P.	1920		
Mrs. Rolf C. Norris	P.	1920		
Sidney A. Berkett	P.	1920		
John E. Atkinson	P.	1920		
Mrs. Elizabeth Atkinson	P.	1920		
Mrs. Alfreda Harrington	P.	1920	Died	1927
Laura E. Hastings	P.	1920		
Marie Isabel Gill	P.	1920	Dismissed	
Mrs. Burton W Libbey	P.	1920		
Louis S. Lunt	P.	1920		
Vernon E. Sanborn	P.	1920		
Margaret E. Scott	P.	1920		
Mrs. Mary A. Sugden	P.	1920		
Harold M. Templeman	P.	1920		

Name		Year	Status	Year
James F. Walsh	P.	1920		
Mrs. Clara Berkett	L.	1921	Dismissed	1926
Mrs. Lillian C. Remick	L.	1921		
Mrs. Cora P. Hutchins	L.	1921		
Mrs. Elizabeth A. Sherlock	L.	1921	Died	1929
Joseph Sherlock	L.	1921		
Dudley G. Soden	L.	1921		
Mrs. Caroline K. Soden	L.	1921		
David Walker	L.	1921		
Mrs. David L. Walker	L.	1921		
Ruth Walker	L.	1921		
Doris Walker	L.	1921		
Leland Buzzell	L.	1921		
Cyrus Stowell	L.	1921		
Mrs. Cyrus Stowell	L.	1922		
Lillian M. Johnson	P.	1922		
Helen V. Brackett	P.	1922		
Laura D. Mitchell	P.	1922		
Mabel L. Stowers	P.	1922	Dismissed	
Hermon C. Brackett	P.	1922		
Frederick Darlington	P.	1922		
James L. Byrne	P.	1922		
Wilfred C. Holroyd	P.	1922		
Arnold Wood	P.	1922		
Ernest Abbott Gaunt	P.	1923		
Chester F. Smith	P.	1923		
Lucy H. Richardson	P.	1923		
Frances M. Archibald	P.	1923		
Dorothy Mae Little	P.	1923		
Albert E. Jewell	P.	1923		
Aroline R. Walker	L.	1924	Dismissed	1926
Christina A. Whittier (Mrs.)	L.	1924		
Mrs. Louisa G. Goodwin	L.	1924		
Rev. Egbert W. A. Jenkinson	L.	1924		
Mrs. E. W. A. Jenkinson	L.	1924		
Mrs. Lillian M. Jewell	L.	1925	Died	1928
Rose Donelian	P.	1925		

Mrs. John E. Davis	P.	1925		
Helen L. Budd	P.	1925		
Dorothy F. Gay	P.	1925		
Elizabeth R. Gay	P.	1925		
Persis L. Gaunt	P.	1925		
Dorothy C. Kimball	P.	1925		
Winnifred C. Paisley	P.	1925		
Barbara E. Paisley	P.	1925		
Josephine (Swain) Waller	P.	1925		
Paul A. Archibald	P.	1925		
Donald J. Bond	P.	1925		
William Budd	P.	1925		
Frank R. Johnson	P.	1925		
J. Freeman Libbey	P.	1925		
David O. Lynch	P.	1925		
Howard W. Sherlock	P.	1925		
William G. Wardwell	L.	1925		
Walter Buchanan	L.	1925		
Mrs. Walter Buchanan	L.	1925		
Jennie M. Marston	L.	1925		
Louise H. Hook	P.	1926		
Bertha E. Lowell	P.	1926		
Ruth S. Rafferty	P.	1926	Died	1926
George S. Baketel	P.	1926		
Harry Buckley	P.	1926		
John E. Davis	P.	1926		
Thomas Longworth	P.	1926		
Mrs. Maud G. Day	P.	1926		
Ruth E. Archibald	P.	1927		
Margaret S. Bend	P.	1927		
Thelma Budd	P.	1927		
Margaret E. Craven	P.	1927		
Alice I. Emmons	P.	1927		
Marion L. Gaunt	P.	1927		
Annie L. Harrison	P.	1927		
Vera Jagger	P.	1927	Dismissed	1929
Evelyn A. Stanley	P.	1927		
Jean B. Stowell	P.	1927		
Frederick J. Hill	P.	1927		
William Longworth	P.	1927		

Elroy F. Mitchell	P.	1927
Malcolm F. Stevens	P.	1927
Lewis H. Conant	L.	1927
Mrs. Lewis H. Conant	L.	1927
Leighton S. Thompson	L.	1927
Mrs. Leighton S. Thompson	L.	1927
Mrs. Mabel L. Stanley	L.	1927
Dorothy Sherlock	P.	1928
Alice Wood	P.	1928
Ernest Lehninger	P.	1928
Wallace R. Marden	P.	1928
Vfilliam Turner	P.	1928
Georgia B. Easton	P.	1929
Helen E. Mitchell	P.	1929
Nettie Harrison	P.	1929
Norman P. White	P.	1929
James Nicholson	P.	1929
George T. Byrnes	P.	1929
Mrs. Edward Archibald	L.	1929
Gladys M. B. Dyke	L.	1929

INDEX

A

Adams, Abraham 24, 25
Adams, Phineas of Haverhill 39
Allen, Jonathan of Bradford
    33, 39, 48
Amesbury, Mass. 18, 20, 21
Anderson, John of Windham 35
Andover Hill 58
Andover, Mass. 18, 39
Andover Theological Seminary
    47, 57, 59, 62, 67, 72, 87, 101
Archibald, Edward A. 97, 105
Archibald, Everett H. 92
Arlington St. 38
Asen, Thomas 17
Atkinson, N. H. 39

B

Bailey, Abner 27
Bailey, Allen 97
Baily, Jonathan 17
Baldwin, Dr. of Boston 50
Bare meadow 12
Barker, Ebenezer 104
Barker, James 17
Barker, Stephen 10, 15, 17, 19
Barker, Zebediah 17
Barnard, John 18, 19
Barstow, Frederick L. 105
Barstow, Thomas, house 38
Bartlett's Brook 29
Batchelder, Mr. of Haverhill 50
Beard, Betsey (Field) of W.
    Brookfield, Mass. 57
Beard, David of W. Brookfield,
    Mass. 57
Beard, Spencer Field 56, 57, 58

Beard, William Spencer 58
Bell, Mr. 31
Benson, Colby 98
Benson, Mrs. Joseph 84
Bentley, William 28, 38
Berkeley St. 10, 38, 90
Beverley, Mass. 50
Binns, John H. 105
Blake, Horace Lyman
    76, 77, 79, 81
Board of Censors 98
Bodwell, Daniel 12
Bodwell, Ella P. 90
Bodwell, Henry 15
Bodwell, Isaac 49
Bodwell, William 53, 54, 56, 104
Boxford, Mass. 39
Boynton, Nehemiah 86
Bradford, Mass. 18, 39, 42
Bradford, Mr. 34
Bradford St. 63
Brook St. 90
Brown, John of Haverhill 20
Buswell, Joshua 69
Buswell, William H. 105

C

Carleton, Edward 104
Carleton, James 42
Carlton, Elijah, horse 49
Carlton's Road 12
Carter, Clark 86
Chapel Cemetery, Andover, Mass.
    58
Chapman, Eliphaz, farm 29
Charles St. 91
Christening Basin 18
Christian Endeavor 101, 102
Christian League of Methuen 96
Clark, Samuel 17
Clough, Isaas 17
Coit, Alfred 87
Coit, John 87

159

160

162

164

ADDENDA

An interesting fact gleaned from the history of a neighboring town tells us that the Haverhill Church did not alone contribute the original covenanters. From *the Historical Manual of the South Church in Andover*, we find the names of the following eight men dismissed by letter on Oct 26, 1729, "to form the church in Methuen": James Barker, Ebenezer Barker, Stephen Barker, Zebediah Barker, John Gutterson, Thomas Austen[1], Joseph Gutterson, and Benjamin Stephens[2]. On the same date, the names of six women were recorded[3]. They were admitted on Nov 30, when twenty-seven more, "consented" to the covenant. The Andover South Church was organized in 1711. The above mentioned, men probably lived in the western section of Methuen. We might expect them to be taxed by the Haverhill Church; and yet some might have lived on the other land; "the strip of land perhaps a mile and a half in width between Haverhill line and 'Drawcutt' line seems to have been granted by the General Court to individuals". (see *A Historical Sketch of Methuen*, by J. S. Howe.) These would have been taxed by the chosen house of worship; the Andover church. The question is often asked as to "where was the home of Christopher Sargent?" Did he have a parsonage "house"? We know not, except from the record cited on page 26, we judge it to have been on the "Commons" near the Meeting-house.